Wit and Wisdom
from the Parents of Special Needs Kids

Lynn Hudoba

Preface

Blog. Blog. Blog. Kind of a funny word. Especially if you say it repeatedly. More so when you're drunk, I would imagine. If blogging had existed sixty years ago, I wonder whether Hemingway and Faulkner would have blogged. J.D. Salinger lived well into the age of the blog and never felt the urge to post a single word.

I'm no Big Papa. But I am Big Daddy. That's the moniker I hide behind when I blog about my fourteen year old autistic son, Griffin. I entered the special needs parent blogosphere in the summer of 2010 and have yet to leave. It is here that I was exposed to like-minded parents who put their stories out there for the blogging world to see.

Much like our children, there is a spectrum of special needs parent bloggers. Some are funny. Some not. Some are prolific. Some hardly ever post. Some are profound. Others, like me, not so much. One thing we all have in common is a love of our children and a need to express ourselves.

When I wrote my first book, *Big Daddy's Tales from the Lighter Side of Raising a Kid with Autism,* I included essays by a dozen of my blogger compatriots. Some allege that this was simply a ploy to fill pages without having to write anything original. Others claim it was just a gimmick to expand my audience base and sell more books. I would vehemently defend myself against these baseless allegations, but I was only allotted 378 words for this preface.

Irrespective of my motives, the feedback I received from all three readers of my book was overwhelmingly positive. In some instances my guests' essays were more revered than my own work. (Thanks mom.) This led me to a remarkable realization. Specifically, it made me realize that I get hungry when I think. It also helped me see that, given the appropriate platform, my bloggy friends could have a profoundly positive impact on special needs parents outside our cozy little universe.

When I was able to get a word in edgewise during one of our conversations, I mentioned this to my friend, Lynn Hudoba. Within minutes, *Wit and Wisdom from the Parents of Special Needs Kids* was born.

The following pages are filled with the words of the best special needs parent bloggers out there. Enjoy. Or don't. Either way, I'm off to get a snack.

F. Lewis Stark (aka Big Daddy) brings his unique view of fatherhood, and the world at large, to life in his first book, *Big Daddy's Tales from the Lighter Side of Raising a Kid with Autism*, as well as on his frequently updated and hilarious blog, www.bigdaddyautism.com. His tales (and cartoons) from the lighter side of raising a child with autism always spark laughter and discussion. By telling funny and off-beat stories from his life, Big Daddy shows that raising a kid with special needs is not all doom and gloom. To the contrary, it can be quite humorous and inspirational.

Introduction

Bubbelehs,

It is said that each child is carefully chosen for us so that we can learn about ourselves, find within ourselves hidden talents, such as patience, creativity, and compassion, or whatever our particular needs are.

They are a gift and they are a challenge.

When I think about what the difference is between raising a child with special needs and raising a child with ordinary needs, the difference comes down to one thing: emphasis.

Raising a typical child requires patience. Raising a child with special needs requires *patience.*

Raising a typical child requires flexibility, especially as it relates to your schedule. Raising a child with special needs requires **f-l-e-x-i-b-i-l-i-t-y**, *especially* as it relates to your schedule.

And first and foremost, raising a child requires a sense of humor, because if you don't laugh when that annoying thing happens yet again, you will cry. Raising a child with special needs requires a **SENSE OF HUMOR** because if you don't *laugh…* you will cry.

What you are about to read is a collection of stories by parents who have learned how to live life successfully and with *emphasis.*

I firmly believe that one of the strongest tools we, as parents, have in our survival kit is sharing.

The very thing you went through yesterday that had you wondering if it's something you did wrong, or that left you feeling like you're the only one who has ever had to deal with this situation, that experience that brought you to tears of stress or fear becomes the very thing that brings you to tears of laughter, when you read it on the page of someone else's blog. You're *not* alone. Others DO know what it's like to hear the same question for the 724th time... this week. Others DO know what it's like to clean the feces off the wall... again.

And if you're very lucky, reading their successful survival techniques will help you master the challenge of raising your child with ***emphasis.***

Read on, learn, laugh, and be inspired by these amazing parents.

B'hatzlachah — good luck — on your own journey,

Bubbe

Bubbe is Yiddish for grandmother. But more than that, *Bubbe* is a state of mind. *Bubbe* is the one who draws all her *bubbelehs* (loved ones) close and nurtures all, makes sure they're well fed, healthy, learn well, grow strong, and are happy. Bubbe's alter-ego is known as Dena Page, a behavior analyst with more than twenty years' experience helping children with autism and related disorders get well fed, become healthy, learn well, grow strong, and be happy. She has been a DTT/ABA consultant since 1992, an auditory integration therapist since 1999, and an Irlen screener since 2005. And most recently, she's been guest blogging as Logan's bubbe at www.livingwithlogan.com.

Less Traveled Roads

By Pia Prenevost

I shall be telling this with a sigh
Somewhere ages and ages hence:
Two roads diverged in a wood, and I—
I took the one less traveled by,
And that has made all the difference

—Robert Frost

There is this famous essay by Emily Perl Kingsley called "Welcome to Holland", in which she compares the difference between parenting a "typical" child and a "special needs" child to planning a trip to Italy, but ending up in Holland and needing to accommodate to a new destination. A beautifully written and interesting analogy, but it also sounds a little too easy. No offense, but Holland and Italy both sound pretty swell to me. I tend to think of parenting a special needs child a little differently.

Parenting is like taking a walk in the woods. Now, most parents hike the well-worn trail. It is wide and well-traveled, with many other parents hiking right along beside them. They see similar overlooks and famous panoramas, beautiful vistas, and mountain creeks. There are definitely hills to climb, bugs to avoid, and the occasional rain storm. And sometimes they unfortunately step in doggie-doo or trip on a big rock. But they have the benefit of many accurate maps, of others who travel with them on the same path and who (mostly) share the same experience.

However for the parent of a special needs child, parenting is different. For you, there is only a very thin trail or maybe no path at all. Grass and tall weeds cover the forest floor. There are unexpected mud pits that suck your shoes in. Your pack can be heavy, terribly heavy at times. There is wildlife galore in this woods, some of it so beautiful and some of it scary and dangerous. Gnatty, swarmy bugs bite. You aren't very sure where you are going or what direction to take, and the few guidebooks or fellow travelers you meet all have a different opinion or direction in mind.

Mostly you hike alone, but occasionally meet others who hike these woods too. They know your hike because they are doing it as well. They can share tips and tricks to making it through the woods. But you must hike on your own, because no one's journey is the same.

Eventually you learn to navigate these woods. Slowly but surely you learn to avoid the mud pits, to defend against the scary critters, and to cut though the tall grasses in order to make the journey go more smoothly. And you hope that you are going in the right direction, and that you aren't going to run into a bear or a mountain lion. You hope for the beautiful vistas, but you are never quite sure where you might end up.

The special needs parent is on the less traveled road.

The trick for survival might be how you approach this journey. Is it a scary, lonely, difficult trek? Or an epic adventure? Do you resent the loss of those famous panoramas and those easier hikes? Or is the possibility of unique delights and experiences enough to make you pull up your hip-waders and find your way through the woods? Do you stay lost, or find your own way? The curse and blessing of being a parent of a special needs child is your own forced growth, becoming more than you thought you could be, or maybe more than you ever wanted to be. You don't have to rise to the challenge. *It is your choice. And yet, is there really any other choice?*

Pia Prenevost writes the blog *The Crack and The Light* at www.thecrackandthelight.com. She is mommy to the Amazing J-man, who has apraxia of speech, autism spectrum disorder, and the longest eyelashes known to man.

Familiar

By Spectrummy Mummy

I notice the girl spinning as we first enter the park. There are two of these spinners at this playground, and they are part of the reason why I'd brought Pudding, my 4 year-old aspie, and her brother to play here. It is a multi-sensory delight, with sand and wood chips, things to climb, places to hide, swing, and, of course, spin. Pudding ran immediately to the unoccupied one. The other girl was spinning at great speed, and not getting dizzy. I smiled at the mother hanging close by, waiting to be needed. That was familiar.

Pudding noticed that this girl had her shoes and socks off, and asked if she could do the same. Cubby ran off immediately to play with trucks. Pudding wanted to start with the swings. Though we had driven straight from an occupational therapy session, she clearly needed more vestibular input.

With my two occupied, I'm at liberty to observe the girl now, who is no longer spinning. She is older than Pudding. Her language seems good as she talks to her mother, but she makes no effort to speak with the other kids playing nearby. She is content filling a bucket with sand, dumping it out, and repeating the process. Before long, her mother sits down and encourages her to make actual sandcastles, like I knew she would. That was familiar too.

I sit down and take advantage of a moment's peace to quickly send their father an email to let him know we can pick him up after the park. My device catches the girl's eye, and she comes bounding over. She doesn't look at me. She is far too close, completely unaware of the boundaries of personal space. All too familiar. I smile at her, and ask if she'd like to look. Impulsively, she touches the screen. Her mother comes running up and apologizes. I tell her there is no need; my own kids touch it all the time. She needs to learn, insists the mother. So familiar.

The girl is reluctant to leave in spite of her mother's insistence. I want to tell her that I understand. I get it. We are the same, she and I, just like our girls. But I don't. The daughter reads from my screen. Her mother is embarrassed. Great reading! I tell her. The mother shakes her head.

"She is *too* good at reading."

Here is my chance to pull out the jargon, to let her know we speak the same language. We are part of the same secret club of parents of kids with invisible disabilities.

"Oh, is she *hyperlexic*?" I ask.

Immediately the mother is taken aback by my choice of word. She is reading two grades above her age, she informs me. Then she looks over, sees Pudding bouncing up and down, and I see the realization dawn on her that I am an affiliate of the autism mothers club. Her turn to parry with jargon.

"This is a great place to come for *vestibular* input."

I tell her that we have just come from OT. I can just say *OT*. She knows. She is familiar. My turn:

"I find that her eye gaze and *pragmatic* language improve after some time on the swing."

She nods in agreement.

Cubby runs in one direction; Pudding in the other. Our conversation is over. I notice the woman looking over and smiling at me from time to time. We don›t get a chance to speak again before we have to leave, but it is okay. There is such comfort in knowing someone I recognize is nearby.

Spectrummy Mummy is a stay-at-home mother to Pudding and Cubby. They live a globe-trotting lifestyle, but the real adventure began when Pudding was diagnosed with an autism spectrum disorder in 2009. She blogs at www.spectrummymummy.com.

Sophie and the Boys

By Claire Roy

"I want that man to kiss me on the lips!"

My then fifteen year old severely physically and intellectually disabled daughter's eyes were glued to the television. A close-up shot of a handsome young singer was on the screen. No question, the kid had good taste in men.

Indeed, Sophie may well be only able to work academically at a grade one or two level, but she is all teenager when it comes to boys. She loves the handsome chiropractor that comes to the house every week to treat her. She gets all misty-eyed and googly when he comes near. At one point, we had a male nurse and all she could do was repeat his name over and over again:

"John! John! John!" Even the refrigerator repair man got the eye.

But, a few years earlier when she was in a combined grade seven-eight class, it was the boys who gravitated toward her. Indeed, Sophie, hardly able to talk or do much of anything, was the girl without cooties. At an age when puberty favors the girls with height and other, ummm, physiological developments, the boys were all over the place: physically challenged size-wise, socially inept, totally lacking in confidence. Sophie was the only girl that didn't scare them. She actually made them feel comfortable. Rotating seating arrangements made it so that a variety of individuals ended up sitting near Sophie that year, and whereas the girls slowly pulled away from her, too busy with their fashion fancies and social agendas, the boys got closer.

One fellow held her hand as much as he could, even while he was doing his own work. He spoke softly to her and got stuff she needed. Another engaged Sophie in a variety of jokes and pegged her with a nickname. She laughed at all his antics and called him "Hayden-potato-head". A boy that the girls loved to hate — macho, built like a brick house and a total smart ass — one day shame-facedly declared quietly to her that he had an alcoholic uncle in jail. During a daytime gym party, the boy rejected by all because of his insufficiently masculine demeanor, asked Sophie, in her wheelchair, to dance. She was the only girl he had ever approached.

Many teens now shy away from Sophie when they see her. They don't know how to act, or what to say. Some feel pity, others are annoyed. I am not concerned, however, as I recall the events of that year: the year the boys took note of Sophie. Here, disability leveled the playing field and two sorts of kids reflected back to each other the simple love that both desperately wanted to share.

***

Claire Roy is "just a mom" of two girls, blogger, disability advocate, and former Montessori teacher, caring full time for Sophie up in the Great White North. She blogs at www.severedisabilitykid.blogspot.com.

Stick To The Script

By Amanda Broadfoot

When I first heard the "A-word" in reference to my now five year old son, I was afraid he would never talk. When we became introduced to the wonderful world of echolalia, I was concerned he'd never say anything he hadn't heard from Charlie Brown.

I had been resistant to teaching him social scripts, afraid he would come off as robotic, without comprehending the meaning of his words. But in the past year, I saw him attempting to make social connections without the tools to do so. Teaching him to say, "Hi, I'm Billy!" to new companions was preferable to hearing him announce, "I think there must be something wrong with me, Linus," again and again.

When his sister, Willow, received a talking Dora the Explorer doll for her birthday, Billy suddenly had scripts for expressing affection. I was bowled over the first time he hugged me and said, "You're my best friend. It's great with a friend like you," until he called me "Boots" and warned me about Swiper. But he meant the friendship words. He still uses them with his close family.

There are all kinds of options for teaching autistic kids social cues and scripts. There are the low-tech "social story" options, in which you create little books with catchy titles like "Happy Hands and Heads" and "What DOES Go in the Toilet."

There are high-tech options like DVDs and apps for the iPad. Billy learns really well from video, so we have a lot of these — with widely varying levels of success. The ModelMeKids "Going Places" app has been very helpful in tackling grocery store visits, haircuts, and eating out in restaurants. The app plays a simple slide show with pictures of a little boy venturing out.

The audio is read in the little boy's voice: "We're going to the grocery store. I stay close to my mom. I keep my hands to myself. It's time to check out!" Each story ends on a positive note with a happy smiling face.

Video modeling gone wrong can be seen in his response to repeated viewings of sumo wrestling videos on YouTube. It took me three weeks to figure out why he was screaming Japanese phrases at me before tackling my knees — though his synchronized swimming routines, performed on his bed, are admittedly quite entertaining.

When I took Billy to the doctor recently, I brought the iPad along, and let him watch the "Going to the Doctor" slide show in the ModelMeKids app. Rather than spend the entire waiting room stint screaming, he happily perused the slides about sitting still for the doctor, letting the doctor examine you, treating the doctor like a friend, etc.

However, we had to sit there so long that he got bored with the "Going to the Doctor" app, and by the time his name was called, he had spent quite a bit of time watching stories about "Going to a Restaurant", "Going to a Playground", and "Going to a Hair Salon."

While the exam involved a fair bit of screaming and, admittedly, an attempted biting, he handled most of it very well. Occasionally, he would whimper phrases like, "The doctor is my friend," in a dubious tone.

After double ear infections were confirmed, biting was avoided, and prescriptions were called in, the ordeal was officially over and Billy was free to go.

With tears streaming down his face, he managed a smile at kind Dr. Singh. "Thank you!" he choked out, waving. "I like my new haircut!"

Suffice it to say, a few of our scripts are a work in progress.

Once upon a time, Amanda Broadfoot wrote movie scripts for a (sort of) living. These days, when she has time to form a coherent thought about motherhood, she blogs about it at www.LifeIsASpectrum.com.

Autism Dad by Choice

By Yuji Fukunaga

I met my son shortly after he turned two years old. Or rather, to be more accurate, shortly after he turned two, I met Kai, the boy who would later become my son.

His mother, Rika, had lost her husband to cancer only a month before their son was born. And with that, Kai lost a father he never knew.

I came along a couple of years later. After many months of grieving and raising Kai on her own, Rika thought she was ready to start dating.

On our first date, she told me about her son. Kai had been a difficult baby. He was upset all the time. He was constantly crying. He did not sleep well at night.

As time went on, she had seen signs that there were issues that went beyond being a fussy baby. He did not make eye contact. He did not respond to his name being called. He lined up toys but did not play with them. He did not speak.

She suspected that her son had autism.

And. a few weeks after our first date, her fears were confirmed. He was officially diagnosed.

Some people consider it amazing that I did not run away right then and there, never to be heard from again. But I don't think that I did anything special. I guess you have to know Rika and Kai to really understand that.

In Rika, I saw a woman who was trying to bounce back from a devastating blow only to be given another one. Through it all, though, she had gained perspective on life. She was stronger than she realized. And, she had a lot of love to give.

When I first met Kai, he hardly seemed to notice that I was there. As I had expected after hearing Rika's description, I couldn't get his attention or get him to engage with me. He just sat on the couch, snuggled against his mother, and watched videos.

One day, I got silly with him. I started jumping up and down on a bed and thumped my chest while I gave a loud Tarzan yell. He smiled. It was the first time I saw him smile. When I stopped, he looked straight at me, rolled his own tiny hands into a ball, and started to tentatively thump his chest. He didn't say a word, but I knew that he was telling me that he wanted me to do it again. And when I did it again, he laughed hysterically. And that became our "thing".

In those goofy moments, I got my first real glimpses of a sweet boy with a playful personality who was just bursting to come out of the shell he was trapped in. I knew right then that I would love being his dad, and no diagnosis of autism could ever change that.

Rika and I got engaged soon after, and we married the following year. I adopted Kai as my son.

Together, she and I learned about autism, and tried to do whatever we could to help our son overcome its harmful effects so that he could enjoy life to its fullest.

We have now been together as a family for more than four years. Kai's personality, the one that I first saw in our silly play, has fully emerged. He is now a chatterbox who exuberantly expresses the many fantastic thoughts that are in his head. His intelligence, so hidden when I first met him, is now clearly visible. He is funny, charming, wondrous.

For most, being the parent of a child with autism is something that is thrust upon them. For me, it was different. I had a choice.

It turned out to be the best choice I ever made.

Yuji Fukunaga is a lifelong Chicago-area resident and dad to Kai, a dynamic 7 year old boy with autism. You can read more about their experiences at his *Hanabi Boy* blog at www.hanabiboy.blogspot.com.

What, No Instructions?

By Kathy Kresin

Autism does not come with an instruction manual. There is not a user's guide or troubleshooting handbook. Of course, there are hundreds of books on the market and when my son, David, was first diagnosed, I tried to read them all, every...single...one. And while I found some to be extraordinarily helpful, I really needed some straightforward advice from a mom with personal experience; tips that did not include words like intervention and regression, sensory or stereotypy.

So, I present to you my top five tips — things that I probably would have found helpful as I embarked on the autism journey.

1. *You CAN do this.* (Cue the Helen Reddy music.) You have amazing strength. Yes, I am partly referring to the Vulcan death grip I developed to stop David from doing things like bolting from the exam room when the pediatrician did not heed David's four minute warning and he then started the unintelligible countdown "hive-hore-three-two-one-year-o." But I am also talking about the strength to trust your own instincts, to be an effective advocate, and to believe that you know your own child better than the experts.

2. *Some people are cruel.* You will need to develop a thicker skin. I am not saying that you should not stop to "educate" the woman outside the restaurant who utters the (she thinks rhetorical) question as you are heading to the car mid-meltdown, "Why don't you just spank him already?" As an aside, you may find occasions when you are happy that your non-verbal child does not have the ability to repeat certain phrases.

3. *Go with the flow.* You will develop skills that you never imagined you might need, like the ability to snooze through the same seven second clip from *SpongeBob SquarePants Lost at Sea,* playing for the 279th consecutive time (briefly considered a military torture technique but later rejected as inhumane), only to wake up when the clip has stopped and it is quiet, alerting you to the possibility of impending shenanigans. And your

ability to identify the source of the clip from the SpongeBob SquarePants corpus that you now own is a testament to the fact that you have not lost your grip on reality — not yet, at least.

4. *Pick your battles.* The big stuff is really big, so you need to learn to let go of some of the little things, like the fact that your son chooses to store his whistle in the knife drawer, steals lanyards from church, or carries around eight rolls of Bounty paper towels every day for a week.

5. *Be Patient.* For the next several years you may have to stop for all doors including, but not limited to, garage, elevator, cabinet, and every door of the frozen foods aisle of the local Super Target — both sides. And then you will need to wait until the door has closed completely without regard to the fact that you may be running late for school/work/doctor's appointment. This experience will be good training because progress will come in baby steps and rewards come in small packages.

Disclaimer: These tips may only pertain to the individual depicted when he is in a good mood on third Sunday of the month and alternating Fridays. Past performance does not guarantee future results. So, please keep your hands and feet inside the ride at all times and wait until the rollercoaster has come to a complete stop before exiting the car.

Kathy Kresin is mom to two boys, the youngest of whom was diagnosed with autism just before his third birthday. She chronicles the surprising joy and day-to-day challenges of their lives on her blog www.ourbutterflymoments.blogspot.com.

Ballet Shoes and Pink Tutus

By Jen Troester

A girl! I was having a *girl,* and I was over the moon. I dreamed of having a daughter. Sharing secrets. Braiding hair. Beaming with pride as she waved a chubby little hand at me during the first of many dance recitals. I couldn't wait. Before she was even born, I had her whole life planned out. Mostly in pink.

And then suddenly, I didn't.

The funny thing is, at first we were convinced Katie was gifted. She hit all her milestones early. She sat up at five months old, and walked at nine months. Who cared if she didn't speak one word? None of the other children had taken their first steps at eight months old. Every kid develops differently. My tiny little genius would speak. I had no worries.

And then suddenly, I did.

It is excruciatingly painful to watch your child get passed by. To listen as her eighteen month old peers sing "Twinkle Twinkle" without missing a beat. My own child couldn't even say the word "star". To watch as she played off in a corner alone, caring not about the other kids or most of the toys scattered about. In a way, I was lucky. She never hit or bit another child. She never tried to steal a toy. She didn't care if someone took one from her.

But, she should have.

I remember her finally saying the word "dog" at the age of two. I was so excited. Then overcome with grief. We felt light years behind.

I knew it was autism all along. Our family pediatrician knew. It took until she was five years old to get a formal diagnosis. All that early intervention missed. All the times at school she was told she was a bad kid. Made to sit out in the hall, not welcome in class at the age of three. The times when I was the only parent left in the school lobby, because my child was having a meltdown. She couldn't put on her own coat, yet had no words to ask for help. So they let her struggle. They lamented to me what a difficult child she was. I cried over how they just didn't get it.

They do now.

And so, my dreams changed. Never will I dress my child for a dance recital. Giggle at the Buddha belly protruding from her costume. I wasn't going to see her dance with ten other toddlers, or search for her hand reaching out amongst the sea of others. There would be no tutu. No French braid. I let it go. Let the dream slip from my fingers. One of many. They just weren't important anymore.

Now I have different dreams. To see her happy, laughing, enjoying the life she has been given. Autism might not be a blessing, but my child is. The dreams have changed, but not the love I have for my daughter. I will take that little hand and guide her. Lead her forward into all the wonderful potential I know she has, even if others don't see it. I will help her realize her own dreams; mine don't matter anymore.

And that's OK.

Jen lives in small town in Massachusetts with her husband, Kai, and their two children, Katie, 7, who has autism, and Ben, their wild child 4 year old. Her blog is *Living Life With a Side of Autism* at www.livinglifewithasideofautism.com.

Sleep Tight

By Ashley Pooser

I held my breath and crept silently into the dark room. Only divine intervention allowed me to successfully navigate the mine field of toys strewn across the floor without breaking an ankle. I knelt by the bed and narrowly missed setting off Buzz Lightyear with his futile efforts to contact Star Command. I took a deep breath and embraced the cliché.

I watched him sleep.

His size twelve feet, which only hours before had connected with my unfortunate ribs when I brought out the wrong pants, were quiet and still. His little hands, long since outgrown the chubbiness of toddlerhood, were wrapped protectively around a treasured tank engine. His face had shed the anxiety of the day and its barrage of sensory input. His four-year-old body was curled into the same position as when he was a baby, and I remembered those nights I spent rocking him. Back when a lullaby and a hug could make everything better. Back before we learned the A-word: Autism.

I watched him sleep.

I was grateful for his peacefulness, however long it would last, and I wondered where he goes in his dreams. Is he riding the rails in some exotic locale? Maybe he's tending his windmill amidst fields of tulips. Or perhaps he's carefully listening to a pair of lungs with his magic stethoscope. Wherever he is, I hope it's a more pleasant dreamscape than last night when he woke up screaming every two hours. When he couldn't tell us what was wrong. When a lullaby and a hug couldn't cut it.

I watched him sleep.

I wondered what it would be like to live a day in his beautifully unique world. A world where ceiling fans are full of wonderment, but toilets are absolutely terrifying. Where he can identify every state on a map, but can't find words through emotions to tell you why he can't eat his sandwich unless it's cut into squares, not triangles. Where the color orange holds some mysterious beauty and the number four is fascinating.

I fear that he is starting to notice his differences. I didn't expect it to happen so soon, but he's always been so intuitive. I wonder how much time we have before we're forced to have The Talk. You know. The one where we have to tell our amazing little boy that he has autism.

When we have to tell him that certain things will always be a struggle for him. I hope we remember to emphasize the good things. I hope we think of the good things. I hope we don't screw it up. The idea terrifies me. I'm just not ready yet.

So for tonight, I watch him sleep.

Ashley is mama to two beautiful stinker babies. Caleb, 5, was diagnosed with autism in 2010, and Grace, 2, was diagnosed with a severe case of the terrible two's. She blogs about the craziness of life at www.stinkerbabies. com.

Blending In

By Karen Asplund Velez

"The only rule is don't be boring and dress cute wherever you go. Life is too short to blend in."

—Paris Hilton

There are lots of things I love about my son's differences from other children. One of the very special things about my child is that he can take something that is seemingly mainstream and put his own twist on it, making it completely unique. In this way, he can covet a new toy just like any boy his age, "want it", and play with it. He almost blends. At least on the surface.

When other little boys want wireless remote control cars to race, my son wants to anthropomorphize them and make them his friends. He does this a lot with inanimate objects. Having had a fascination with boulders, he somehow became obsessed, not with climbing them or learning about their composition, but rather about making sure they had something to drink. The larger boulders all had to have apple juice. The smaller boulders needed milk.

Having moved from boulders to cars, he transferred this need to quench thirst from the boulders to Vipers, Mustangs, Challengers, and Jeeps. He was particularly enamored with a large blue remote control Viper. He desperately wanted it for his fifth birthday and would talk non-stop about it day after day. Whenever he brought it up, he never talked about racing the car, washing it, gassing it up, or changing the tires. He called it "Thirsty" and wanted to ensure that it had enough apple juice.

In a similar vein, my son has a rock tumbler. He loves the tumbler and begged and begged for me to purchase a refill so he could use it again. Like a lot of kids on the spectrum, my son was relentless in his pursuit of the elusive tumbler refill kit. Finally, the big day arrived. The rocks were here! Excitedly, I supervised him putting them in with the grinding grit and water, sealing the barrel, placing it in the tumbler and closing the lid.

We agreed to take the tumbler to the laundry room, as far away from the rest of the house as possible. The little guy ran and skipped to the laundry room with me. Jumping for joy, my happy little guy pressed the on button. This was the big moment he'd been waiting for. The obnoxiously, loud sound of tumbling rocks, and a motor the decibel level of a lawn mower, began. Thunk, clunk, clunk.

Instead of walking out and asking me a thousand questions about how this would smooth the rocks, what we could make when they were done, or how long it would take, my son began to dance. Smiling at me with big dimples and swaying from side to side, my little boy was happy. Apparently, this was his version of "rock" music.

If it makes him happy, I'm happy too. At least I didn't have to fill the tumbler with apple juice and milk. Shhh, I don't want to give him any ideas.

Karen Asplund Velez lives in Northern California with her husband and her exceptional son who happens to have autism. She is a civil trial lawyer whose work, fighting for the underdogs throughout her career, was good practice to advocate for her son's needs. You can find her at her personal blog, *Solodialogue* at www. solodialogue.wordpress.com.

Full Moon Fever

By Kerry Ann Butler

I have a tribe of other autism moms and for that I am thankful. Mainly because I am free to mention something that, if I did in the "normal" world, other mothers would think I had totally lost it. But with my tribe I can say something like, "The full moon makes my son crazy." And I am immediately bombarded with validation.

During the week of the full moon, I can almost guarantee that Kyran will act "bat sh*t crazy". Sorry for the swear word, but "bat poop crazy" just doesn't do it justice. For the sake of not swearing, I will call it BSC. By definition, BSC is just that: running, crashing, jumping, maniacal giggling, and not so much sleeping. My son is the master. He will come home from school and I can tell by the way he is laughing and throws his backpack in the general direction of the hook that the full moon is coming and we are in for some BSC.

It's fascinating to watch, if I weren't so worried about emergency room visits and my couch's shot springs. His energy has no limits and if BSC could somehow be bottled and sold legally, many autism families' financial worries would be over. Most adults would pay big money for that kind of energy. I know I would.

The parents? We're exhausted and we hate the full moon. The tribe has a choice name for her as well, but I will let you use your imagination for what we call her. I will give you a hint: she is as old as her profession. She is the reason my sweet boy will wake up at 2:00 a.m. laughing at her and then me because I actually say, "Go back to sleep. It's still nighttime." There is no time for sleeping when the moon is full and BSC-time is to be had. He is exhausted too, but can't help it. The next day at school he pays dearly for his short night. But by the time he is home again, he gets a second wind and, lucky us, BSC kicks in again until he finally passes out later than usual. The cycle ends as the moon finally becomes completely full and starts going the other way. We are relieved as he dials it down a notch or two, but all too soon that week arrives again and we start the process all over.

Usually with Kyran's teachers I am professional and rarely share any theories like BSC and the full moon. But his teacher this year is wonderful and if I could I would drag her with him up through the grades. We email nearly daily about Kyran's days. For that alone, I heart her big. I mentioned one morning that Kyran was loopy and had been up since 3:00 a.m. because of the full moon. Then I hit send and thought, "She will think

I am nuts for that." Not only did she not think I was nuts (thanks, because I think I am most days) but wrote back a very long dissertation about her full moon theory and autism. More validation.

And so with that validation, I become bolder. One day the following month, I was out on a run and saw Kyran's speech therapist who was also out for a jog. Again, always professional, and she has been his ST for the last four years at school. It was a Sunday and we were both dripping sweat and wearing lycra, so therapist/parent barriers were down. She asked about Kyran. I said, "Oh, it's the SUPER full moon and he is all BSC at home with Dad right now." And then I waited because not only had I mentioned the moon but I had also sworn. She started laughing and couldn't stop. I'm pretty sure she wants to be friends now.

Why is this important? The fact that Kyran's teacher and ST think I am hilarious? Not even close. It's that autism moms are brilliant. We are submerged deeply in this with our kids and have each other's backs. We come up with these theories from observations and discussions. It gives us confidence to share what we know with the "normal" world. We can help others learn about our kids. We can help doctors, therapists, and educators with our kids. Someday it won't be so odd to ask autism mothers what we think in helping all children. So with that hope, I share the full moon theory and BSC knowing that our tribe just grew larger.

Kerry Ann Butler was born and raised in Seattle, but soon she and her husband Paul, their 18 year old neurotypical daughter, and 7 year old son, Kyran will be moving to Arizona. Kerry Ann and Paul co-author *The Butler Way* at www.butlerway.com. Both are avid runners and encourage others to get out there.

Identity

By Christine Zorn

When autism entered my life, it hit like a ton of bricks. It became all-consuming and entered into every aspect of my life. I ate, breathed, and slept with autism – really, I would wake up in the middle of the night thinking about it. It took over and became the primary part of my identity. I was the mother of a child with autism. I talked about it. I cried about it. I read articles and blogs about it. All. the. time.

Part of this was due to feeling that I had to find something, anything, to help my little girl Samantha. I felt that if I was not doing something or thinking about something autism-related, then I was not doing enough for my daughter and that I was not being a good mom to her. Well, it turned out that I couldn't keep living like that. It was mentally, emotionally, and physically exhausting. On top of it, it wasn't any fun at all – not for me or for the rest of my family.

I had lost my identity. I had lost the person that I had been before autism hit. I saw myself primarily as the mother of a child with special needs. At one point during all of this I had a mini-breakdown in front of Samantha's early intervention teacher. I sobbed and spilled my guts, telling her how completely stressed and unhappy I was. She explained to me that I had to look at Sam's needs in the context of my entire family. I needed to ask myself if what I was doing for Sam was also what was best for me and for my other children. As obvious as that may sound, I had not thought of things in those terms. It was quite a revelation

Since then I've been coming around to a new way of thinking about our lives. It's a process and it takes a lot of work. It definitely hasn't happened overnight. I see that I need and deserve an identity other than "the mom of a child with autism". Although that will always be a large part of who I am now, I deserve to have other interests that make me happy and contribute to who I am as a person. I have many roles and interests. I am Sam's mom, but I'm also a mom to my other two kids. I'm a daughter. I'm a friend. I love dogs. I love to sew and create. Occasionally, I like to cook. And once in a while I even like to read a book that isn't about autism.

For me to have an identity besides "a mom of a child with autism" is good for Sam too. If I'm happy and physically and mentally healthy, I am a better parent to her and much more capable of giving her what she needs.

I frequently hear parents of children with autism say that they don't want the autism label to define their child. As a parent, I don't want to let the autism label define me either.

Christine Zorn lives in Minnesota with her three children and two dogs. Her 3 year old daughter, Samantha, has epilepsy and global developmental delays and was diagnosed with autism at age 2 1/2. Her blog is *A Sugar & Spice Life* at www.asugarandspicelife.blogspot.com.

Blindsided

By Lou Tecpanecatl

Parents of children on the autism spectrum become some of the most formidable advocates for a number of reasons. Since the social and cognitive delays associated with the disorder can be misunderstood, we are often-times put in a position to explain or defend our child's actions and behaviors. However, being able to success-fully argue your case to the school board at the yearly Individualized Education Plan (IEP) meetings is always a challenge.

Diego, my oldest son, has autism and just recently turned five years old. Since he is in his final year of preschool, we recently met with school officials for his "Turning Five" IEP meeting to discuss his transition into the elementary level of special education. My immedi-ate concern was for the continuation of all of his current therapies, and that his IEP for the upcoming school year have a set of clear and challenging goals that would propel him forward. The morning of the meeting, feeling intently focused, I walked in with my binder of progress reports, tagged in many places to highlight my arguments and a list of detailed goals I wanted included in his plan.

Imagine my surprise when early on in our discussion the psychologist started to focus on the alternate assessment clause of the IEP. This would excuse him from taking standardized tests a few years down the line, allowing him to be tested separately in a way that accurately measured his skills. The psychologist from the board of education actually said that if we continued on that path, Diego would receive an IEP diploma and we could forget about him attending college. What?! I was abruptly separated from all of my thoughts on his needs for kindergarten and forced to look ahead, many years down the line.

We had just been blindsided by something that was not appropriate for this or any other meeting, but because of the implications I felt obliged to answer. As I started speaking, I felt a powerful surge of emotion so I paused to try and compose myself. I was inundated with memories and images of the last five years as Diego struggled to learn to communicate. I saw scenes of him screaming, crying and then vomiting from feeling nervous and scared when therapists tried to interact or place demands on him. So fearful of the pending exam and due to his sensory processing issues, he had the same reaction during visits to the pediatrician. I pictured my wife sneaking out the front door to go to the store, because if he saw her leave he would be inconsolable. Once she left he thought that she would never come back, and that was hard for me to watch.

I realized that the school official was using one of the most powerful forms of persuasion against a special needs parent; prey on their concerns and anxiety about what the long-term future holds for their child. Fighting through the anger and uneasiness of the moment, I calmly explained that no one could possibly know how Diego's skills would improve in the next six months or even during the upcoming school year, let alone ten to twelve years down the line. Those few moments of reflection that had immediately followed the psychologist's hurtful comment ended up becoming my launching point to successfully argue for the inclusion of a majority of the goals I had written prior to the meeting.

Yes, our son is developmentally delayed, but he also happens to be an intelligent, funny, and remarkable little boy. In fact, just two days after that intense IEP meeting we were getting ready to leave for his music therapy class when he stopped, looked up at me, and for the first time in his life said "Daddy".

Lou Tecpanecatl is the father of two boys and his oldest son was diagnosed with autism in 2008. He shares his family's story to help create a better understanding of the disorder that despite its prevalence is somehow still referred to as "invisible". His blog is *Our Life With Diego* at www.ourlifewithdiego.blogspot.com.

A School Crush

By Cheryl D.

My daughter is seven years old and has Asperger's Syndrome. She's had that label since she was four and a half years old, although she showed signs of it when she was as young as nine months old. Because of the Asperger's, my daughter has a difficult time handling transitions or anything else that doesn't go her way.

When she was younger, she'd have huge tantrums over little things. For example, she would tantrum over dropping half a grape on the floor. I'd have to replace it with another half of a grape. If I tried to replace it with two halves, she would tantrum more.

On the plus side, she is very smart and loves to learn new things. She taught herself to read when she was four, and started reading science articles in *National Geographic Explorer for Kids* soon thereafter.

Her preschool years were particularly difficult, but not for the reason you may be thinking. My daughter *loved* school. She loved it so much that she never wanted to leave. Every day when I'd pick her up, she'd start to tantrum as soon as she saw me because she didn't want to leave school. Ever.

I was getting tired of these theatrics, so one day I decided to give her some perspective and show her that she really didn't want to stay at school after all. When she refused to leave as she always did, I said "Fine, you can stay. I'm leaving! Bye!" As I slowly walked away, waiting for her to catch up to me, I realized I couldn't hear her coming. I turned around and saw that she was exactly where I'd left her. "Bye-bye, Mommy!" she happily called out to me with a huge smile on her face. Well, I guess she called my bluff!

Another time when she didn't want to leave school, she asked why she couldn't just live at school. It had everything she could ever want or need. I asked her where she would get food, and she replied that the school had a kitchen. I asked her where she would sleep, and she answered that she would sleep in a comfy beanbag chair in her classroom. I pointed out that all her toys and books were back at home, she shrugged and said school had lots of books and toys too. She had everything figured out. In fact, she made a pretty persuasive case for living at school.

Now that she's seven, my daughter still loves school. However, the behavior therapy she's received has helped her make a lot of progress in reducing her rigidity to situations outside her control and helping her to handle transitions. When I come to pick her up from school, she's happy to see me and races over to give me a big hug. Best of all, she's happy to go home with me and hasn't expressed any interest in living at school. Yay, progress!

Cheryl D. shares the hilarious exploits of raising her daughter with Asperger's Syndrome at www.littlebit-quirky.blogspot.com. She likes to spend her free time, such as it is, reading other blogs, cooking, watching television, and working part-time at an internet company.

Like Mother, Like Son

By Amanda Griffiths

When I dreamed of what my children would be like, I dreamed they would be like me. They would get good grades in school. They would like to play sports. They would be involved in other academic activities after school as they got older. I never dreamed of the word autism.

Autism has been a funny little word in our house. My oldest son was diagnosed later at age eight and a half. By this point I had realized that this child is me, only more intense. But he is me. Does that put me on the spectrum too? This is a question that my son's diagnosis has made me ponder often.

We both have clothing sensory issues. This is a big one. I distinctly remember one outfit I had that I abhorred, but everyone kept trying to get me to wear it. The seams bothered me, and so did the tag. I would not wear it. Then one day, I tried it on and it was fine. I can't tell you how many times I've gone through this with my son. We also both share the hatred of seams on socks. I've mostly outgrown mine, but his is still very much alive.

We both have food sensory issues. Please, no Jell-O, pudding, or anything soggy or slimy. And for the love of Pete, please don't let our food touch on our plates. Again, I'm not so bad now that I'm older, but I still don't eat Jell-O or pudding. Soggy bread is the absolute worst in food sensory issues. My son and I both agree on this.

He does like sports, but only noncompetitive backyard sports. I'll take it. He's not the little jock I dreamed of, but that's OK. I've turned into a delicate flower in my old age, and would prefer to not freeze during spring soccer season when it could still snow, or sweat like I'm in a sauna during summer baseball games. Unless he chooses a nice climate-controlled indoor sport, I'm OK with staying home.

My son is smart. Too smart for his own good sometimes. Our biggest issue in school so far has been making sure that he's challenged, because the literal thinking of autism keeps his test scores just under where they need to be for certain enrichment programs. I can't tell you how many teachers I've had to say "I told you so" to because they let my son get bored, left him to his own devices, and he made a bad choice.

My son also questions authority. At home, this makes my blood boil. At school, I think it's absolutely awesome. I too was that kid saying, "Why do we need to learn this?" or "What is the importance of that rule?" or "When will we use this material again?" I don't think I was doing it in elementary school, but rock on, kid.

Are these all traits of autism? It's hard to say. Does this mean I'm on the spectrum too? I don't know. I do know that autism or not, I did get a child like me.

Amanda is a thirty-something stay-at-home mom of two boys on the autism spectrum, and Army wife of eleven years. She writes at *Confessions From HouseholdSix*, at www.confessionsfromhh6.com, to try and maintain what sanity she has left.

The Third Degree

By Dawn Hentrich

At a birthday party recently, I had an ~~excruciatingly-painful~~ educational conversation with someone's grandmother; a well-meaning woman with too much foundation and a penchant for conceding to her granddaughter's every whim. Everyone should have one.

Before talking to Granny, I had been sharing the finer points of cupcake consumption with a pre-school special education teacher. Invariably, it came out that Ben has autism. Not that the head-shaking, hand-flapping, sensory-craving behavior he was displaying didn't give *that* one away. But while we don't intentionally advertise, neither do we hide from it.

When the teacher wandered off, I paused in my cupcake feasting while my son proceeded to fulfill all his sensory needs by turning the bouncer into a violent inflatable tempest of bruises. At which point Grandma took her cue to engage me in conversation.

Now I'm not chatty. Nor social. I don't like people, generally. But it *was* a party.

Anywhoozits, she struck up a conversation with me because the host had mentioned me once or twice because this was, in fact, the birthday party of my son's BFF. Or as much as kids with autism can have a BFFs. They hug. That's close enough.

Meemaw smiled, engaging me in idle chit-chat. "What do you do? How do you know BFF? Lovely weather we're having." And then, WHAM! "What exactly *is* autism?"

sigh

Turns out the bundle of whiny "pay attention to me" pre-teen in pigtails next to her was as typical as they get, so this woman had never been exposed to a kid, or anyone, with autism.

And, you know, bless her heart for actually asking instead of sitting there making assumptions and half-wit observations. I proceeded with great caution to lay out a definition – lack of social skills, sensory and play issues, language – covering the basics, emphasizing that each person with autism is very different, and trying not to overwhelm her with too much information.

And then it came: The Look. Some of you may know it. The "bless your heart but thank God I'm not you" look. It's often accompanied with The Whisper – the "if I don't say it too loud then it won't really touch me and I won't have to think about it" whisper. Yeah, the one that makes you want to ask them loudly if their herpes cleared up. *That* whisper.

At which point my kid proceeded to pummel her granddaughter. Seriously, this kid has got some *timing.* In his defense, it *was* a bouncy house. He was not the only boy pummeling others, and all he really did was bounce into her. Repeatedly. But it was enough for this drama queen to exit the bounce house with much over-the-top caterwauling.

So, condolences given to the girl, my son was brought before the panel of angry frowny-faced adults, and apologies were forced out of him. And with no more than a backward glance, he returned to the cage match in the bounce house.

When I looked at the Grandmother again, with her pinched lips and judgy eyes, I wanted to tell her, "*That* was autism." It's the not knowing how to really play together and sometimes craving that strong sensory element even if it causes pain. And it's apologizing by rote, without eye contact, because he doesn't really understand what he did wrong.

She may have learned a little that day, and this emphasizes the most important lesson. It's okay to ask about autism. It's the only way any of us learn. So ask and tell as much as you like. You don't even have to whisper. But save the judgmental looks for the caterwauling drama queens.

Dawn Hentrich is a snarky, maladjusted, misanthropic stay-at-home mom who cares for her amazing and hilarious 4 year old son Benjamin between blogging, laundry, and happy hour. You can read her rants on her blog, *This Side of Typical*, at www.thissideoftypical.com.

Pure Love

By Kelly Hafer

I hold my son's still nap-toasty hand as we walk together down the stairs.

He had just finished his nap and was once again ready to roll. Immediately upon waking today, like every other day, he happily called for me: "Momma, I took a good nap! Momma, I took a nap for *you!*" Equally refreshed, I trotted upstairs to collect my boyo. Once he heard my footsteps on the stairs, his excitement increased. "Momma, Momma! I so proud of you, Momma. I took a nap!"

After I reached his bedroom, I gave him permission to push open the not-so-childproof gate he had already unlocked. He looked up at me, gave me the patented Teddy smile, and rushed out of the gate and gave me a brief, yet self-driven, hug. He's ready for juice, he said.

This scene may not sound like anything special or out of the ordinary for parents to experience, but for us, parents of a child with autism, this daily routine is nothing short of miraculous. A miracle derived from dedication, hard work, and nearly three years of multiple therapies. Our son has had to work and fight for every single bit of success in his life. Nothing has ever come easy for him. He has had to fight from his very beginning.

Our son entered our lives when he was not yet two years old. And although many children within the foster care system have difficulties with attachment, transitions, and reaching developmental milestones, we knew relatively quickly, once he was permanently in our home, that his struggles were different. More extreme. Unending.

Ted refused to make eye contact, would not accept our touch, and screamed as though skin was being peeled off of his body for hours upon hours at a time. At twenty-two months old, he only spoke five words, and those he did speak were barely intelligible or used incorrectly, and proved unhelpful in ultimately determining his wants or needs. He was non-compliant, unable to follow even the simplest of directions, and, God bless him, the most uncoordinated little boy we had ever seen.

But, oh, his smile.

His smile did us in.

There were times when we questioned whether or not we had what it takes to be his parents; whether we were the best option available for him. We wondered if we possessed the fortitude to deal with the daily struggles; if we could handle teaching and re-teaching him literally every single thing that he would need to learn to prepare him for life. We doubted ourselves and our therapists. But we never had a chance. Ted's smile proved mightier than his limitations.

Three years and hundreds of therapy appointments later, Ted has learned to make eye contact – or at least a close facsimile. We work on conversation skills, speech, occupational, and physical therapy. We see a developmental pediatrician, a pediatric neurologist, a psychiatrist, and child psychologist. We've worked our way through a pretty substantial list of medication options, done multiple EEG's, MRI's, and CT scans. We've done copious amounts of blood work and genetic testing. We also had an unfortunate experience with a not-so-scrupulous chiropractic neurologist.

And yet, Ted smiles through it all. His smile continues to melt even the hardest of hearts. Although he still will only accept affection given on his terms, the rare moments that he offers tangible proof of love to us – a quick hug before running away to play or scooting just a little closer on the couch – are absolutely the purest displays of love ever experienced.

Kelly blogs at www.UnplannedTripToHolland.Blogspot.com. She writes about her experiences as a mom to three children, two of whom are somewhere on the autism spectrum, life as a military spouse, and the unbelievable, yet true, craziness that is her life. She enjoys long moonlight walks, cheesy romance novels, and copious amounts of rum.

The Little Things

By Tanya Savko

"Years from now, we'll look back on this and laugh."

– Common refrain of many autism families, including mine.

I love to laugh. My DVD collection is dominated by comedies, and my favorite thing to do in Vegas, although I've only been there twice in the last twenty years, is to go to a comedy club. In lieu of trips, I watched stand-up on Comedy Central every Friday night for years.

My older son, Nigel, was diagnosed with autism at age three in 1997. Back then and for a few years after, his autism was rather severe, and there wasn't a whole lot of funny. But I was right in thinking that there would be things I'd look back on and laugh about. There was the shrieking while cutting his hair at home, wondering with dread when Child Protective Services would darken my doorstep. I can laugh about it now. Then of course there was the time I had to run over to stop him from squatting and pooping on a park walkway because his extremely sensitive hearing made him shriek in public restrooms, so he avoided them. There were several people around; I was mortified. But I laugh about it now.

Now, Nigel is sixteen, and due to years of intensive therapy and dogged determination (mostly on his part), he has slowly evolved into a milder state of autism. But he has also developed a seizure disorder. And I wonder, as I reflect on last week's 2:00 a.m. seizure – hearing his body banging against the wall, leaping out of bed and running to his room so I can make sure he's not being strangled by a twisted sheet, finding the door locked, dashing off to the tool box to get the multi-head screwdriver only to find that it was not in the box because, as usual, Nigel had taken it to work on a project, realizing the screwdriver was there in his locked room, probably a few feet away from his seizing body – I wonder now, will I look back on this and laugh?

I thought it showed strength of character to be able to let things roll off my back, to not wallow in self-pity about the challenges I faced. I thought that laughter was how I could get through it. And yes, it helped. But I realized it wasn't just about being able to see the humor in hard times. It was okay to acknowledge the difficulties and let them be. Because I figured out what else I really needed to do. I needed to appreciate what was already there – the enjoyable moments, the endearing exchanges. Like when Nigel comes to me as I'm sitting at my desk and stands there, holding something small in his closed hand. He says in his deep, flat voice, "One thing that's different about me is that I notice little things that other people would find insignificant. Like this rock, which is shaped like Sri Lanka." And he opens his palm to show me a smooth, dark gray, undeniably Sri-Lanka-shaped rock.

I smile, trying not to laugh because he is so beautiful in his seriousness, and I tell him that he's right. About the rock, and about noticing the little things. And I realize that, as an autism parent, that's exactly what I do, what I've always done. *I notice things that other people would find insignificant.* Those are the things, funny or not, that get me through the long days. They're mine to cherish, my life richer because of them.

Tanya Savko is the author of *Slip*, a novel about going through a divorce while raising a child with autism. She lives in southern Oregon with her two sons, and is also the author of the blog TeenAutism.com.

The Gift

By Jenny Herman

I sat there, trying not to cry. I didn't want to upset my son, who had just given me a precious gift. Tears welled up in my eyes, striving to push out and spill down my cheeks. "I must not scare him," I thought. "Don't ruin this fragile moment. You know if you say or do too much, he'll melt away." I smiled at him, praising his efforts. He had just completed a rite of passage.

I held it in my hands and knew exactly what I'd do with it. Times were more than tight, so I could afford only a cheap dollar store frame. I wrapped it up, eagerly waiting for the next morning so we could surprise my husband. I'm sure I was more excited than my son.

I placed a lot of pressure on this simple gift. I hoped it would erase some of the hurt autism had inflicted on my husband's heart. Autism often steals affection and desire for emotional intimacy. There was a long time when my son wanted almost nothing to do with his father. Daddy would offer to read a book to him. No. How about a game? No. Requesting a hug? You're joking, right. Not a chance.

While other dads tickled and tackled their boys, my husband watched his son line up toys. Other men played trains *with* their sons, laughing and making sound effects together. My husband helped my son create elaborate train tracks so the trains could go around and around and around without any social interaction whatsoever. Rejection daily mocked my husband as he watched his little man grow.

I'm sure my husband was surprised when he opened his present that Father's Day. Our little man had never created anything like this before. I thought it was the perfect gift. That drawing sparked something in my son. He has since created picture books and more detailed drawings. He's not a professional by any means, but he clearly loves to draw, and I think he'll be pretty good someday. Maybe in the future he'll draw a real portrait of my husband, one that is accurate and looks like a photograph.

Something tells me it won't mean as much as the portrait he got in 2010: the simple circle with psychedelic looking eyes, crooked mouth, and missing nose. That awkward drawing was my son's first-ever face drawing. More importantly, it was the first time my son drew "My Daddy."

Jenny is a wife, mom to two boys, freelance writer, and autism advocate in the Metro-Detroit area. She blogs about the good, the bad, and the amazing that autism brings her way at www.manyhatsmommy.com.

Losing Control

By Jennifer Bush

The other day, my husband Jeff was watching a documentary about stress. Although I wasn't paying close attention, I heard enough to know that we humans have an intense physical reaction to stress (similar to that a zebra has when chased by a lion), that it affects things like how fat is deposited on our bodies, and that it is killing us.

Just what the mom of an autistic child wants to hear.

I'm well acquainted with stress. Most days I feel completely spent by the time my kids go to bed. My schedule is packed with therapies for my son Moe, participation in an autism research study at Stanford, taking my two year old to music and mommy and me classes, not to mention things like laundry, grocery shopping, blogging and going to the gym. Even those last tasks, the ones that are meant to be stress *reducers,* often add stress because of the time they takes away from other things I feel like I should be doing.

Sometimes I have to wonder what is so tough about my life. Moe is in school most of the day and we've got a pretty good routine. I have babysitters to watch my younger daughter when I need them. Moe is non-verbal and quite rambunctious, but generally happy. And other activities, like blogging and going to the gym, are things I do because I enjoy them. Am I just a complainer?

It turns out that one of the major causes of stress is a lack of control. As someone who is well acquainted with the term "control freak," this comes as no surprise. But I never before pieced together that this lack of control is what is so stressful about being the parent of a special needs child, especially one with autism. We are not in control; autism is.

After diagnosis, we coped by going into action mode. We researched, got assessments, lined up services, and set out to kick autism's butt. We tried to take control. Slowly we learned that, although these things help, therapy can only do so much. Development has to happen on its own and this can be slow or fast, happen in trickles or bursts, but is almost completely out of our control. And that is stressful.

But relinquishing control can also be immensely freeing. When we first started sleep training Moe, long before he showed signs of delay, we would put him down in his crib, say good night, and walk away. Yes, it was hard to listen to him cry, but there was also relief in knowing that I didn't have to *do* anything. Moe needed to learn to sleep on his own. And it worked. In a few days, he learned to soothe himself to sleep. You can't force someone to sleep, so why beat yourself up trying?

Maybe it is the same with Moe's autism. I can't force the autism out of Moe any more than I can force his curly hair straight. And those curls, such a surprise when they first appeared, now seem so integral to Moe that it is impossible to imagine him without them.

Perhaps this is my first step toward true acceptance of Moe's diagnosis. I may never love the challenges that autism has brought to our lives, including the return of some pretty serious sleep issues. But I can stop fighting for control, and that might make things just a little less stressful.

Jennifer Bush lives in Silicon Valley with her husband and two kids, including a preschooler on the autism spectrum. She has degrees in Sociology and Communications from UC Berkeley and an MBA from Yale. You can find her at her personal blog, *Anybody Want a Peanut?* at www.wantapeanut.com or on Twitter @wantapeanut.

Thunderstorm

By Rhonda Logan

When you think thunderstorm, you think cool lightning. Roaring thunder. Rain pounding against the windows. Some people like to curl up with a blanket on a rainy night. Oh, not so in this house of raging-autistic-teenager-with-aggression-issues!

Thunderstorms here bring a *lot* of anxiety. The first, most detrimental thing that can happen is the power going out. The second would be the cable going out. Tonight brought us *lots* of lightning. One bolt was big enough to give us a power surge. Funny how things fall into place. It's like an emergency exit plan in case of fire.

My younger neurotypical daughter gathered up the dogs and high-tailed it to the basement. I started moving furniture. In between wrestling remotes out of his hand – because he wanted to turn the volumes up to MAX – we started this game, "Who's taller?" It's been weird for me because he's actually taller than me. I get on my tippy toes and tell him "Mommy's taller!" He then is on his tippy toes "Tommy is taller!" Dad joined in tip-toeing around the living room like ballerinas. This goes on for about an hour.

While they're engaged in their dance, I am running back and forth checking on the dogs and child. "TAG YOU'RE IT!" Hubby runs off to get a cup of coffee in the kitchen while I play I'm-the-tallest-ballerina. Tommy gets another remote. I snatch it. He swings. I catch his arms mid-air. He swings around to bite me. I ninja-move my way out of it. WHEW! All those mornings at the gym are paying off!

Within the hour, the meds have kicked in. We're calm enough to actually change rooms. Funny how we're in a tornado watch and heading upstairs to bed. ROU-TINE!! ROUTINE!! We're laying in mom's bed because it's the safe place. We're counting the pauses between the lightning and thunder. As the pauses get longer, he gets more relaxed. It's 10:23pm now, and he is asleep. This all began around 7:30pm.

I thought of being a lot of things when I grew up. A police officer. A teacher. But never ever did I dream that I'd be the Tallest Ballerina. My feet hurt. Next on the agenda is a foot rub from the hub.

Rhonda is mother to a 16 year old autistic boy, a very typical 14 year old daughter, and three pugs. Somewhere in the middle, she has a husband. She blogs about life as she sees it at www.pugariffic.blogspot.com.

Autism Makes My Stomach Churn

By Grace

I have many neuroses. Far too many to list here, but I will tell you about a few.

I've struggled with shyness my entire life. I've made great strides in overcoming this, but it still pops up in my twisted mind every so often. To this day, I hate walking into a room full of people I don't know.

I hate being the center of attention and have always done my best to fly under the radar. I had low-level anxiety my entire wedding day. Fortunately, I didn't even have to show up for court on my divorce day, so I didn't have to endure everyone's scrutiny twice.

I really hate to perpetuate gender stereotypes, but I'm an extremely emotional creature. I've been known to cry at credit card commercials.

And I have this irrational, overarching fear of making a nuisance of myself. I guess I was told I was a pain in the butt a few too many times during my childhood, I don't know. I could spend thousands on therapy trying to figure it all out, but I have better things to spend my money on, like Ritalin and wine, so I have just accepted this as fact and done my best to roll with it.

I'm far too timid. I'm a terrible networker. I hold myself back. I'm my own worst enemy sometimes. Because of my numerous phobias, I've been overlooked many times in my life by many people.

Here's the thing about being a special needs parent, however: If you meekly maintain a low profile, your child will get nothing. NOTHING.

This whole autism thing has forced me to step outside of my comfort zone so many times I don't know where the boundaries lie anymore. If I had my druthers, I would just resume a quiet, unassuming life of being as agreeable as possible, and have everything my son needs dropped in my lap. But hoping that might actually happen would make me even crazier than I already am.

Because of autism, I have had to walk into rooms full of unfamiliar people clutching official reports detailing my son's deficiencies and *not* disintegrate into a hysterical blubbering mess. I have had to ditch my "be agreeable" philosophy and adopt a much more demanding one in order to secure the services my son needs. Instead of waiting patiently for a response, I have been forced to leave voicemails for professionals over and over again until someone *finally* called me back. I have become one of *those* parents and barraged my son's teachers with emails demanding updates about his behavior and academic progress.

I have, on rare occasions, just said *screw it* and taken my son to a family-friendly restaurant, knowing full well he wouldn't be able to sit still for more than three seconds. If you happened to be sitting near us, I apologize for being such a nuisance, but autistic kids and their moms need to eat sometimes, too.

I have had to reach out to people I barely know and say "Hey, you have more experience at this whole special needs thing, do you have any advice for me?"

And I have had to ask for help. This is still incredibly difficult for me, but I do it because I have to. I can't do this alone. No one should have to do this alone, but knowing that doesn't make the asking any easier. I ask, however, because I have no choice sometimes. I ask, even though it still makes my stomach churn.

Grace is a smart-mouth goddess and the proud mother of Ryan, who is obsessed with Star Wars, Legos, and farting. Despite what her name may imply, she tends to trip over things a lot. She blogs at www.ThatsRightI-SaidItDotMom.wordpress.com.

Letting Go

By Elizabeth Givler

It was time. My son was finally ready to go to camp. We went to family camps before, but now it was time for our boy to go alone. My husband and I were excited about his step toward independence.

I was not as apprehensive as I anticipated. I was more excited about his weekend away. It would boost his self-confidence. The leaders, who were recreational therapists with our local Easter Seals chapter, knew my son from prior events. He was in good hands. We began to prep my son.

"Ben, you're going on a vacation – without us!"

"Oh, you mean, with Matt [his brother]?"

"Nope, Matt is working. You will go all by yourself."

"But how? I can't drive!"

"We'll drop you off, then pick you up when it's over. You'll be gone two nights."

"Oh."

Pause. He smiled really big.

"Well, sorry Matt and Ellie [his sister] and Mom and Dad, I am going somewhere else to live!" He didn't sound upset about this at all. We said, "Only for the weekend!"

We talked about camp—the things he'd do, the fun he'd have, and the friends he'd make. We told him that we could hardly wait to hear about it when we picked him up. He was smiling the whole time. Preparation was done. Or so we thought.

On our way to camp, he asked, "What airport are you taking me to?"

"We're not going to an airport, sweetie."

"But this is vacation! That means I get on an airplane."

"Oh, no, this is a driving vacation. Besides, this is only *your* vacation, remember? I wouldn't take you to an airport and leave you all by yourself."

"A driving vacation?"

"Yes."

"So will this be very long? How long will it be to drive?"

The time keeping began. Sigh.

At camp, he was supposed to take at least two pairs of shoes, in case it rained. He only wears his sneakers, so I threw in his swim shoes that he wears to the beach. I figured that he could wear these in the shower and to go puddle jumping.

As we continued our drive, he gasped. "Oh! I got my swim shoes, but I forgot my swim suit and my swim shirt!"

"That's okay! You're not going swimming, remember?"

"Oh. Hmmm. So I'm just supposed to *get naked* and wear only my swim shoes?!?"

"IN THE SHOWER!". I exclaimed because I really didn't want him to walk around naked.

"Oh. Well, um, I don't like it."

"Fine. You don't have to." He had to be completely naked in the shower, or have his complete swim outfit on. All or nothing. That's my boy!

When we arrived, he ran to the check-in room.

"Where's Grandma and Grandpa?"

"They're not here."

"But this is vacation. Vacation means that Grandma and Grandpa come."

"Not this time, this is YOUR vacation."

"Oh, okay. See ya!"

I did manage to get a few hugs and kisses before I left. I had mixed emotions about the camp thing. I was pleased that he understood so quickly. I was a little sad that he was so ready to get rid of me. I was happy that he was becoming more independent.

As I drove home, I reminisced about how far he had come, from being non-verbal and having meltdowns to being in regular education and going to camp. I imagined what life could be like in a few years. My boy really could be independent and like it. I'd like that, too. It was time to begin letting go. And that was okay.

Elizabeth Givler is a wife, mom, teacher, writer, blogger, speaker, and entrepreneur. She has three children, two of whom are on the autism spectrum. She blogs at www.autismfromthelighterside.wordpress.com.

I Swear This Kid Is Running Trials with Me

By Jill Herschman

Jacob, my 9 year old with autism, is currently in this phase where he is absolutely obsessed with the time. He asks me at least thirty times a day what time it is. Then he wants to know if it's AM or PM. Then he'll ask again about two minutes later. And then he'll ask if it's AM or PM. And repeat. Repeat. Repeat.

I've bought him at least three watches, which he either refuses to wear (he doesn't like having something on his wrist all the time) or has immediately lost somewhere in the house. As such, the subject of the time and our schedule is constantly being discussed. Constantly.

Lately, though, when he asks me these questions, he then repeats himself, but in a really weird way that seems so familiar to me...

Jacob: "What time is it?"

Me: "It's 5:46"

Jacob: "*WHAT* time is it?"

Me: "5:46."

Jacob: "Good."

Does that not sound like a discrete trial to you? I so remember this from our Applied Behavior Analysis (ABA) days of yesteryear. There is a request (SD). I'm providing the answer (R). My answer is being confirmed (SP). I get my reward in the form of verbal praise (SR).

He does this all day long. Every day. I figure this is some kind of karmic payback for forcing him to endure fifteen hours per week of ABA for two straight years. I'm not sure what skill I'm attempting to master with this process; most likely we're working on getting me to respond to him with *the correct time*, because if I had said it was 5:45 I would have been reprimanded. No M&Ms for me for giving the wrong answer, that's for sure!

Jill Herschman blogs at www.yeahgoodtimes.blogspot.com because lots of random stuff goes through her head throughout the normal course of the day, and she needs a place to put it. Mostly she just rambles incoherently about nothing. She also curses a lot.

*Our Lives Are Sh*t*

By Elizabeth Aquino

It's August in Manhattan and everything stinks. The heat bounces off of the buildings all day, ricocheting from the asphalt, trapped, so there's no relief at night. Outside, everyone is sweaty, clustered at the tops of the subway stairs, waiting for the last minute before descending into the furnace, the whoosh of air as it assaults you on the way down.

Michael and I are lying, flat on our backs and spread-eagled with nothing touching in our double bed on the fifth floor of our walk-up on West 73rd. We have no air-conditioner; the only window in our bedroom is a three-foot square door that opens up onto a tiny asphalt-floored balcony.

Sophie is screaming her head off in the port-a-crib next to the bed. She has been screaming on and off for hours and it's about 2:00 am. We've taken turns trying to console her, walking back and forth, back and forth on the balcony, her body a rigid, sweaty bundle of disconsolate nerves. I'm thinking it's the drugs, as usual, the side effects that are "rare" except when we give them to Sophie. The neurologist has warned us that she might be "irritable." I'm obsessed with this remark. I sit up in bed.

"I can't believe she said that the drug can cause 'irritability', Michael", I say. "More like psychotic. I mean she's psychotic, right?"

Michael is just lying there, his eyes closed. He murmurs in assent, a skill he's perfected in the last year as we've struggled with Sophie's neurological problems.

"I mean, do you think we're killing her with this drug? Should I call the doctor now, and just tell her we've had enough? It's 2:00 in the morning but I don't care. I think I'm going to call her. I can't stand it."

Even though I'm exhausted, mentally and physically, and it's so hot that we can barely breathe, my mind is working frenetically and I'm particularly obsessed with solving things despite the hour. I can't believe that my husband can just lie there, listening to Sophie scream yet not feel the same urgency.

"Please, Elizabeth. It's 3:00 in the morning. We can't do anything now. Just go to sleep." He reaches up and feebly pats me on the shoulder. He thinks that I tend to exaggerate. Sophie is still screaming and I jiggle her crib, a little too hard.

"How are we going to do this, Michael," I say to the room, "Keep this up. Take care of her for the rest of our lives?"

Michael sighs and tells me once again to lie down, go to sleep. Just as arbitrarily as she had started, Sophie stops screaming. The silence is almost paralyzing and makes us more aware of the thickness of the heat, the muffled horns outside the window, the hum of other people's air-conditioners. I close my eyes, stunned.

Out of the darkness, like words in a cartoon bubble hovering over us, Michael's Swiss-German sing-song voice intones, "OUR LIVES ARE SH*T."

The laugh that bursts out of me then is less a sound than an embodiment of all the world's absurdity, including my own. And then we are both laughing, shaking, holding each other, trying to shush so as not to wake the baby.

Elizabeth Aquino is a writer living in Los Angeles with her husband and three children. Her work has appeared in several literary journals, *The Los Angeles Times* newspaper, *Spirituality and Health Magazine* and two anthologies, *A Cup of Comfort for Parents of Children with Special Needs* and *My Baby Rides the Short Bus*. Her 16 year old daughter Sophie's struggles with a severe seizure disorder and developmental disabilities is the inspiration for much of her writing along with the shenanigans of Sophie's two brothers, Henry (aged 12) and Oliver (aged 10). Their chaotic lives are chronicled in Elizabeth's blog, *a moon, worn as if it had been a shell* at www.elizabethaquino.blog-spot.com, along with Elizabeth's periodic rants about politics and the health insurance industry, as well as her love of poetry and gallows humor.

Mompetition

By Heather St. Clair

One of the most annoying things about being a parent is what I call the "mompetition". From birth, parents are already trying to beat each other with the best labor and delivery story – who sweated the must bullets and who went medication-free. Then it's the comparing of the stats – weight, length, Apgar scores.

Honestly I didn't find it annoying at first. In fact I was probably one of the annoying parents always starting the comparing conversation. I was so proud of my son's four hour all-natural birth. I was so proud of his Apgar scores of 8 and 9. I was even prouder when he started crawling at five months and walking at nine. I loved to tell everyone about how he could do "The Itsy Bitsy Spider" with me.

I probably started to hate the mompetition when my son suddenly stopped talking. Or when he started banging his head on every surface he could find. I know I hated it by the time he was four and not potty-trained.

To continue to compare my child to typical children was just setting myself up for a road of anxiety, stress, depression, and late-night margaritas. It's not to say I don't ever wallow in those feelings, but I knew I had to let it go.

The other day in a waiting room I watched a young mother with her toddler. She looked at me and said, "He's just starting to talk! It's so much fun!" I peered over my magazine and said, "Yes, that's a fun stage. My son is in that stage too." The other mom eagerly scooted to the edge of her seat ready to engage me in a round of mompetition and said, "He can count to three!"

I responded, "That's great. My son counts to twenty and he can also count backwards." I didn't add, "Don't interrupt him when he does, because he then will do it thirty-seven more times before he feels satisfied."

She crossed her arms, "My son is showing interest in the potty."

I replied nonchalantly, "Mine is potty-trained." I may have forgotten to add, "After three years of going into the bathroom on regular timed intervals, reward systems, and okay, he still has some BM issues."

She started to look a bit angry. I could see she really wanted to beat me at something. "Well, my son can sing his ABC's."

I put down my magazine. "Brian can repeat every line from any Disney movie. And the other day out of nowhere he yelled 'Go away. Don't want none.' to the unsuspecting neighbor at the door."

Most parents would just shut up at this point. She wasn't having it. She shook her head and said, "There is no way your son is the same age as mine. How old did you say he was?"

"He's seven."

She looked bewildered and said, "But you said he was the same age as my son."

I stood up to leave and said, "No. I said he was at the same *stage* as your son. Mine has autism."

She looked mortified at that point as she struggled to send some sort of apology out between breaths.

I wasn't looking for an apology or for someone to feel sorry for me. I just realized I still had that competitive streak and dammit, I wanted to brag too.

Just because Brian hits those milestones later than others, it doesn't mean I'm not going to brag. In fact it gives me more reason to brag. So "nanny-nanny-poo-poo", my son beat yours today. In my mind, he beats him every day.

Mompetition....live on!

Heather St. Clair is a single mom living on the coast of Maine raising two incredible boys, one of which happens to have autism. She is a recent college graduate, mother warrior, Facebook addict, and writer of *The A-Word*, www.livingwithautism-brian.blogspot.com.

299.0

By Amy Downes

If you have a child diagnosed with autism you know what this is. For the rest of you, it's the diagnostic code in the DSM IV-TR (Diagnostic and Statistical Manual of Mental Disorders) for autism. It's a code none of us wanted, but then for many of us, had to fight the schools to recognize in order for our children's needs to be met.

I know these codes. I know them very well. As an addictions and mental health nurse we diagnose, medicate, and treat based our patients. Sometimes we have more than one code. 315.32 for Expressive Language Disorder, 314.01 for ADHD, 300.00 for Anxiety Disorder. But these numbers and labels are not the only things that define us as human beings.

I used to feel that these codes were like the numbers we assign prisoners. Once sentenced and sent to prison, you lose your name and all that makes you an individual. You lose your identity. You are no longer a father, writer, husband, or son. You are prisoner 543728.

I think initially I would have told you that the diagnosis of both my boys on the autism spectrum was like a prison sentence. Sometimes when they struggle to communicate and live in our "neurotypical" world, they are prisoners to their diagnosis. But I have to remind myself that it's not what defines them. They are both diagnosed with 299.80 Pervasive Developmental Disorder Not otherwise Specified (PDD-NOS). They are only the same by their number. They are both unique and brilliant individuals.

Bryan is such a gifted reader. He loves science and wants to be a marine biologist when he grows up. Sean has the most beautiful singing voice and perfect pitch. His smile is infectious and will melt your heart. He started out signing, but he is now speaking in sentences. They both can conquer a video game like a pro. I just can't believe all the games they figure out and make look so easy.

One thing I have learned about them both is that right when I think I have them figured out, defined, and "coded", they remind that they are constantly changing. They can't be coded and totally figured out. Some changes are positive and some are negative, but that is all a part of their growth and development. Once I allowed myself to let go of the desire to "fix" them, it made life so much sweeter. Acceptance, above all else, is what matters the most. You can't code or label love. You just have to give it; no matter what the circumstances.

So instead of Amy Downes, mother of two boys on the autism spectrum 299.80, I would rather be Amy Downes, mother of Bryan and Sean, the two most awesome kids you will ever meet, who, oh by the way, are diagnosed on the autism spectrum.

Amy Downes is a registered nurse, wife to Rob, and mom and advocate to her two boys Bryan and Sean. Her blog is *Not a Real Princess (Except to My Boys)* at www.notarealprincess.blogspot.com.

Glitter Fixes Everything!

By Lisa Gallegos

I live deep in the trenches of autism. I eat, drink, and sleep autism. A few years ago when we first got the diagnosis, life seemed dismal. I think most parents feel that way at some point. The days when your child is non-verbal, self-injurious, and not sleeping are the times when you hate what has been dealt to your family. Even on those days, I wouldn't take it back. But I wish I had the knowledge of glitter sooner.

There was a week of utter chaos and unthinkable sorrow. I sent my son to school and just crawled back into bed, wishing the world would stop spinning for five minutes. I remember it was a Friday, the day he would bring home his art projects from the week.

I suppose up until that point I had always loved his projects. Much of it was the same cute artwork that my other children had brought home when they were in preschool. But I guess this particular week was glitter week, because when I opened that backpack full of his projects and pulled them out I was showered with a ton of glitter.

It was everywhere. While I was sitting there staring at it, Racer came into the room and said "Mommy, you're so shiny." It was those simple words in the midst of a horrible week, and all the glitter, that snapped me out of my funk.

I called one of my dearest friends and shared my glitter with her. Without her, sometimes I can't see the funny, the glitter of it all, because even though there is always sweet with the sour, finding that "sweet" can be hard to do alone.

What I would suggest to every mother, father, or grandparent dealing with autism, or any special needs, is to find your glitter. Hold it in your memory, use it when you feel at your weakest, and smile. Because even if this week is the worst it's ever been, you will always have the glitter, the stuff that makes you shiny. Then find friends with whom you can share your glitter; friends who need it. Autism can be very lonely, but it doesn't have to be.

Lisa is the Mommy over at The Yuckmouth House, where she watches over her seven kids, two dogs, and a hubby. When she isn't raising a child on the spectrum, dodging mood swings from her child with ADHD, and everything in between, she blogs and prays for sleep. You can find her at www.racersmommy.blogspot.com.

Persistence

By Lizbeth Cole

I would like to thank my great friends at Cigna Insurance for reminding us that ALL of Alex's therapies are no longer in-network and we have to find all new providers.

I would also like to thank Cigna from the bottom of my heart for denying his speech services. I know that pronouncing "R's" are overrated, and reading and understanding social cues are not all that high on the food chain.

That being said, when we started seeing a new speech language pathologist, I didn't like the results of our first meeting. I mean, she's a great therapist and all, but I didn't like the results of the tests she performed. It was a bit like shock therapy for me. And, you know, I like to live in a town called Denial, so it was a little hard to have the results slapped around in my face.

Back to the testing. The first test involved showing him pictures of people, specifically their faces, and he was to tell her what they were feeling, their emotions. Sounds easy, right?

She shows him a photo of this little girl, sitting down, arms wrapped around her knees. She's cowering, afraid. He looks at it, looks at the therapist, and says, "She's angry! See, look how her arms are folded." He points to her arms, happy that he got the first one right.

Another photo of a woman, clearly elated, over-the-moon happy. He takes a look at it and says, "She looks OK." The therapist asks if he'd like to add anything more. "Nope!", he says, clearly happy with his progress.

The next photo is of a woman again. This time she pissed off. Clearly madder than a hornet. Exaggerated eyebrow furrow, fist out, finger pointing, mouth in a wicked grimace. "That's easy!" he says, "She lost something and she's pointing to it!" He's super happy, clear in his mind he's got this thing nailed. You could see him say "I'm a ROCK STAR" in his mind. He was that proud of himself.

I could tell you of all the other photos with pictures of people with squishy feelings that he had to describe, but I won't. I was so upset. Devastated. There I was sitting on the other side of the mirror watching him. He didn't understand what he was seeing, what was so clear to me. He missed them all.

But he was so proud, so happy. He was answering and getting them right! He was proud. Confident. How do you burst that bubble?

I didn't. I put on my I-must-remain-strong-but-I'm-gonna-lose-it-later face.

I think it's a face we all wear. As a mom with a kiddo on the spectrum, I just take for granted how much we have to do to support our kids. How we have to pull them up, be strong for them, and advocate and protect them when they don't have the skills or ability to do so. It's just something extra I heap on at the beginning of the day and take to bed with me at night.

I think that's why I get so fed up when someone has the stones to say, "Oh yeah, my kid does that too." Like they're downplaying him, all the extra stuff I have to do just to get him through the day. I just want to lock them in my bathroom with the iTouch and let them listen to his one song for six hours and say, "Well, does your son do that?"

Now this is something I don't do for my other two children, and it gives me pause. I often wonder, am I doing all of this for Alex to the exclusion of the other two? I wrestle with that every day.

We went to Dairy Queen to celebrate. Because in some ways it was a celebration. At the same time last year he knew two emotions – happy and not so happy. So he's getting there. I get it, I do. I just thought that we were a lot further along than we are. It was so painfully obvious how much further we have to go; he has to go. And it is because of that I am upset.

It was so hard to sit there and look at what seemed to obvious, so clear to me yet was blind for my son. All the facets of human emotion that run through a person's face every day and to him it was a blank slate.

What we do when we're there is work for him. He leaves exhausted. Confused and exhausted. It's one area he does not excel in. He doesn't understand it; doesn't understand how everything else is so easy and this is not.

So I put on my face and we went to Dairy Queen to celebrate. Celebrate how far he's come. Not how far we have to go, but how much progress he's made to get to this point.

All the rest will come in time but right now I'm going to enjoy my ice cream with my son, because that smile of his, that's all I really need.

Lizbeth Cole has four children, three of which are with her, and one in heaven. Her oldest was diagnosed with Asperger's Syndrome what seems like ages ago, and she can only hope the other two can be half the kid he is. Lizbeth used to work as a health care administrator, but now stays home with her children. She loves her kids, but there are some days when she asks herself "What in the heck have I done? I gave up my day job for *this*?!?" She blogs at www.four-sea-stars.blogspot.com.

Parenting and Asperger's Challenges

By Claudia George

When my son was diagnosed with Asperger's Syndrome, it was already the general consensus among the family – his paternal grandparents, his father, me – as well as close friends, that he was autistic. From everything we read we knew he fit the mold, so to speak.

I did not cry really when I found out. I don't recall getting overly emotional on having this vital piece of information confirmed by professionals. I found I just felt more able to start making decisions, rather than just waiting in limbo for what I could do to get life moving. Our resourcefulness and our determination to help my son has really shined in spite of our differences.

I am divorced from my son's father, so being a two-household family rearing an autistic child can be very challenging. I am sure that we are not the only family in this situation, but it adds quite a different dimension of issues.

Routines are not very different between the households, but behaviors my son learns to see as acceptable are very different. In my household, it is not tolerated that he destroys things when upset but I know it happens at his father's or grandmother's home. Some behaviors are the same in all children; they learn what they can get away with and with whom.

The other challenge is the different levels of sensory overload he deals with. At my house, it's a very one-on-one situation. My son is not challenged and his comfort zones are not pushed. I am not saying I don't challenge him but the lack of noisy siblings, other family members, and a larger place create a safety net or a buffer. This means less learning to deal with added stimulation.

In this case, I am grateful that my son encounters this at his father's house. His father remarried and had a second child, who is incredibly active and gives my son some added stimulation, companionship, and someone to depend on as he gets older. Unfortunately for my ex-in-laws and my ex-husband, it creates more meltdowns in their household to have two children, one autistic and the other not.

I always question if I am doing the right thing for my son. No one knows the perfect way to raise any child so I just try to do it with love and patience, as much as I can.

My name is Claudia. I am a single mom but I don't identify with the stereotype of one. I see myself as an independent woman, raising an autistic child, and working on living fully. My blog is *The Story of C...* at www.c-writing.blogspot.com.

Stuck in the Middle with You

By Alysia Butler

A transcript from a pre-bedtime conversation in my house:

My 9 year old son: Mom, so I'm trying to decide between buying the Lego Star Wars "Battle for Geonosis" set and a different one that comes with a landspeeder. The one with the landspeeder comes with an exclusive mini-figure but the other one...

Me: Hold on a moment, sweetie. *(turns to my 5 year old)* HEY! STOP DRAGGING YOUR LITTLE BROTHER AROUND BY HIS ARMS!! *(turns back to my 9 year old)* I'm sorry. You were saying?

My 9 year old: I'm trying to figure out which Lego Star Wars set to spend my money on. I really like them both, but one has more pieces than the other and...

Me: One more second. I SAID STOP!! YOU WILL HURT HIM IF YOU PULL HIS HAIR!! *(again, back to my 9 year old)* Okay, say that again?

My 9 year old: Never mind. I know that dealing with them is more important. I'm used to it.

I have three boys, ages nine, five and two. My five year old has sensory processing disorder and was diagnosed with autism spectrum disorder at age three and a half. Every day I'm caught between balancing his needs against the needs of his brothers. He's sandwiched in the middle of two "typical" siblings. I'm constantly sacrificing one child's needs and wants in favor of another.

I know that every parent with more than one child runs into this. The more children you have, the more difficult the logistics become. But when you have a child with special needs, the balance becomes more difficult. It's not just about how to get one kid to piano lessons while the other one is at soccer. It's about how to get my son the necessary services he needs to survive in the world versus the extracurricular activities my other children desire.

Do I drive an hour for occupational therapy or do I attend my older son's last baseball game? Do I sign my son up for a much needed social skills group or volunteer at younger son's preschool?

It's choosing to move quickly through the bedtime routine for the other two kids because my middle son needs me in his bed so he'll fall asleep.

The guilt is tremendous. You want to believe that you'll do anything and everything to help your child with special needs. The reality is that it's not always financially, physically, or emotionally possible. And the more kids you have, the more intense the guilt becomes.

Me: (to my 9 year old later that night): I'm sorry that I wasn't able to listen to your Lego Star Wars dilemma earlier tonight. I was afraid that your brother was going to hurt someone or himself. Sometimes I just have to step in with them, even if I'd rather be talking with you.

My 9 year old: I know, Mom. It's okay. Can I tell you about it now?

I hope that someday my kids will understand that we did our best to help them – all three of them. I hope they'll see that we tried to figure out what each of them needed at that moment. I hope they know that whatever we did for them, we did out of love.

And most of all, I hope they learn how to help each other. Because I'm ready for someone else to take over.

"Well I don't know why I came here tonight,

I got the feelin' that somethin' ain't right,

I'm so scared in case I fall off my chair,

And I'm wonderin' how I'll get down the stairs

Clowns to the left of me, joker's to the right

Here I am, Stuck in the middle with you

Yes I'm, Stuck in the middle with you"

– "Stuck in the Middle With You", Stealers Wheel

Alysia is a stay-at-home mom living in Massachusetts with her husband and three boys, ages 9, 5, and 2. Her middle son has sensory processing disorder and was diagnosed with autism spectrum disorder in December 2009 at age 3 ½. She currently writes at *Try Defying Gravity* her personal blog, at www.trydefyinggravity.wordpress.com, recounting the joys and challenges of raising three boys. Her work has been published in *The Boston Globe* and *Bay State Parenting Magazine*, and online at *Mamapedia*, *Autism Speaks*, and *The Thinking Person's Guide to Autism*. She is also a monthly contributor to *Hopeful Parents*, and is an editor and writer for the *SPD Blogger Network* website at http://www.spdbloggernetwork.com. You can also find her on Twitter at @trydefyinggrav.

A Social Butterfly

By Wendy Bailey

When I first began to grasp the extent of Butterfly's challenges – ADHD, multiple food intolerances and allergies – I decided to homeschool her. Now, you can't just sit a kid like this down and give them dry book-learnin'. That is *so* not going to take. This is where Butterfly became the leader, and I the follower. If she was interested in something, like a butterfly on the lilac bush, a bee in a flower, or birds swooping and squawking in the Beech trees, that's what we learned about, but in only the detail it took for her to flit, like a butterfly, to the next point of interest. I noticed that she best remembered the things she saw and could continue to visualize. So there was always the possibility I might get away with reviving an interest later by printing up a coloring page and information sheet from an educational website for her.

Butterfly liked bees. She was afraid of them, but she was intrigued too, so she actually learned quite a bit about them – about how they pollinated our garden and made honey with the nectar they collected. One sunny summer day, Butterfly, her Nanna (my mother) and I were standing on the deck watching the birds and bees, literally. We were standing just above one of my flower gardens and a honey bee was busy at work, his tiny backside just visible as he ducked in and out of a little flower. Mom pointed it out to Butterfly and said, "Look Bud, that bee is gathering honey to take back to its hive."

Butterfly gave her a rather disdainful look and said, "Oh Nanna, bees don't gather honey. They gather nectar and take it back to their hives. *Then* they make honey out of it." The look on Mom's face was hilarious. "There is nothing quite like being corrected by a six year old," she said.

Mom knew the facts, of course. She just didn't get maudlin about details, preferring to cut to the chase, especially with a little kid. But there are no short cuts around Butterfly. Facts are facts, and they have to be spoken accurately. It turned out this trait is often associated with Asperger's Syndrome. Aspies are typically very into correct detail once they learn it, to what some might consider a ridiculous degree. In fact, this was just one ongoing behavior that clued us in to the likelihood of Asperger's. Tests confirmed our suspicions.

Explaining social language to Butterfly has always been challenging. Aspies just can't read between the lines, as it were. One advantage we do have is a gaggle of supposedly "normal" relatives whose own social skills are...um...wanting? An example is the cousins who attend family events, but never mingle. They just hang around alone together in a corner, while grand aunts and uncles point them out and ask someone else, "Who are *those* people?" Then there's the aunt who greets people with questions like, "What happened to your hair?" I have, on several occasions, taken Butterfly aside and told her, "What they're doing? Don't do that." And with her aunt, I suggested that she *not* retort "Nothing, what's wrong with yours?" no matter how sorely tempted.

Butterfly is eighteen now, and many socially awkward moments later, she's a voracious reader and a well-informed individual with a consuming interest in music. You still don't want to get any facts wrong around her, because she *will* correct you. I mean, there is no hair too fine to split. And while demonstrating what *not* to do has been useful, it still doesn't help her feel comfortable with small talk. It just doesn't interest her. Nor does it help her take what other people say less literally, although she does get obvious sarcasm and has learned that sometimes people just aren't all that nice.

You know, if I had a magical potion that would help Aspies with social nuance, I'd not only be better able to help Butterfly, I'd probably get rich too, which would be cool. Alas, no magical potion. Aspies...you just gotta love 'em.

Wendy Bailey is mom to Butterfly, who has multiple food intolerances, ADHD, learning challenges, and Asperger's Syndrome. Wendy raised and schooled Butterfly with the help of Len, her husband and Butterfly's dad, and her mom, Kathleen. An online friend asked questions about her experiences and suggested that Wendy blog about them. The resulting blog is *Raising Butterfly* at www.raisingbutterfly.blogspot.com.

Expecting the Unexpected

By Pam Byrne

With a swift kick to my ribs, I was wide awake at 3:00 am. Eight months pregnant with Alex, I knew that since I was awake, I might as well go to the bathroom. Once I got there, an unmistakable gush meant that my water had broken and labor had begun, three and a half weeks earlier than expected.

Thinking I had more time to prepare, I had not packed a suitcase yet, nor had we put together his crib. After awakening my husband and phoning my parents, we headed off to the hospital uncertain of what was ahead of us since this was our first child, who would also turn out to be our only child.

Because I had developed an autoimmune bleeding disorder, my pregnancy was deemed high-risk, which meant a flurry of activity and an insistence by my obstetrician that I have a Caesarian section under general anesthesia. Although we were disappointed that we wouldn't see Alex being born, we were thankful that the birth was safe for both of us, and we thought we had smooth sailing once the pregnancy was over.

Even though Alex was born nearly a month early, he weighed almost seven pounds, earned good Apgar scores, and had fully-developed lungs, thanks to the Prednisone I had been taking for my condition. The first year, he made all of his major milestones – such as creeping, crawling, and walking – within the typical ranges. Moreover, he was a happy and alert baby who ate, slept, and interacted with people well. We felt blessed to have a child who was so good-natured and healthy.

As time passed, we noticed that he seemed oddly fascinated with words and numbers, preferring birthday cards to birthday presents and patiently sitting through credits of movies, mesmerized by the words on the television screen. While Alex had an affinity for written words and was beginning to read, his speech was not developing normally and we became concerned. Despite the reassurances of his pediatrician that speech delays are typical in boys, we continued to watch him closely and hoped he would start talking soon. After spending months trying to potty train Alex, I began to suspect that something was terribly wrong, and my mother's instinct knew it was autism.

Shortly after his fourth birthday, we took Alex to be evaluated through our school district, and after much paperwork and many tests, they determined that he did, indeed, have autism along with hyperlexia, a rare condition in which children learn to read before the age of five. Knowing that Alex had been reading, we understood why he preferred words to images and why he liked studying my old college textbooks, which had no pictures. Just as he had entered the world early, he had mastered reading on his own earlier than most children. Speech and toilet training were other matters, and he would develop those skills on his own timetable, as well.

Through the years we have learned that Alex must always do things on his terms when he's good and ready. Progress for him isn't always linear, and it certainly doesn't follow the patterns outlined in child development books; however, progress always eventually comes, often when we least expect it. For us, life with autism has meant learning to wait patiently and celebrating successes when they arrive – essentially a matter of always expecting the unexpected.

Pam Byrne is the mother of a son, Alex, who was diagnosed with autism in 1996, at 4 years old. She writes twice-weekly entries for her blog, *One Autism Mom's Notes* at www.pambyrne.blogspot.com.

Making Friends

By Patty Porch Hooper

My son Danny struggles with making friends. Not uncommon in autism, I know, but it is heartbreaking to me nevertheless, especially in light of how fiercely he wants a friend. Danny enjoys being around other kids, but he isn't very good at communicating appropriately with others. It's definitely not for lack of trying, but his quirks often get in the way of making connections with others his age.

And those quirks have also brought him ridicule from others at times, being called "retard" by a kid at the park and "weird" by a classmate. More often than not, though, rather than ridicule, kids just choose to ignore him because of his differences.

The older he gets, the more his differences seem to matter to the kids around him. I worry that he'll always have difficulty finding someone who accepts him for who he is. My fear is that he will feel lonely and isolated and friendless.

This past week I had the opportunity to help out at Dan's school's Carnival Day. Danny was delighted when I informed him I would be at school.

In charge of the beanbag game, I watched as groups of kids swarmed the building, talking, laughing, and having a great time. Some kids moved from station to station on their own, while others stayed with their friends. As a girl from church approached my station with three friends, all of them holding hands, Danny watched them intently. He then moved towards me grabbing my hand in imitation of them, and he greeted the girls.

I could see on his face that he just wanted to be like them, like this girl from church, who he considers a friend, but who doesn't really associate with him at school. My heart lurched as he futilely tried to get these girls' attention and approval. They ignored him completely and walked away.

I tried to forget the incident and focus on how happy Danny was that I was at school with him, but I couldn't shake the disappointment and hurt that I was feeling on Danny's behalf.

Later, a boy approached me and said, "Hey, you're Mrs. Hooper, aren't you?"

Surprised, I nodded and asked how he knew me. He said, "You're Danny's mom! Danny and I play all the time."

The boy was Holden, the one boy in class that my son occasionally talks about. Though Danny had mentioned that Holden often played with LEGOs at recess, I didn't know if the two boys actually played together or did any substantial interacting with one another.

Holden enthusiastically informed me that he and Danny played together a lot and that they enjoyed themselves enormously, so I suggested that we have Holden come over for a play date. Both boys were thrilled and Holden gave me his phone number on the spot.

Holden then turned to Danny and said, "Come on, Danny! Let's go play a different game." Though Danny had spent much of the afternoon at my station hanging out with me, he joined Holden without hesitation.

At the end of the afternoon, when the kids began filing back into their classrooms, I saw a sight that brought tears to my eyes. Danny was walking and talking with Holden while they shared a bag of popcorn.

What might have been a completely ordinary, even mundane sight for a parent of a neurotypical child, had filled my heart with hope and joy. Out of the blue, Danny had made a friend all on his own with no prompting or coaching. And it felt like maybe everything would be okay after all.

Patty Porch Hooper is a stay-at-home mom of three. Her oldest son has autism and Sensory Processing Disorder. Before kids, she taught high school in Chicago's inner city. She chronicles her family's adventures in her blog *Pancakes Gone Awry* at www.pancakesgoneawry.blogspot.com. She has also contributed to other sites, like *Hartley's Life with 3 Boys, Our Journey THRU Autism,* and *The Thinking Person's Guide to Autism.* Her latest project is starting a LEGO social skills group for kids on the autism spectrum in her town.

Autism Is Serious Business

By Michele Hughes

Autism is serious business. It's tough around here; definitely not for the faint of heart. But then again, we do get our share of laughs out of it as well.

Like when I took them out to play in snow so deep we could barely walk. Even my then two year old twins gave up and started crawling again. My oldest autie boy, Big Guy, takes off running for the swings, no problem. It caught up with him though, as later on he threw up and decided to lie down on the snow to recuperate.

Or like at an Autism Family Day at the stables during a horse ride. Three-quarters of the way around, he decided to jump off and run away. Toward us and not another horse, thankfully. I was waiting, and laughing.

Or when Hubs took three of the olders, including Big Guy, to mini-golf and decided to hit golf balls afterward – something I would have discouraged and only heard about afterward from my tell-all aspie children. Big Guy took off running, right into the grassy area where the balls were getting hit. A chase ensued – my tall, skinny kiddo sprinting away with his father and aspie brother running after him, shouting for him to stop. Then Hubs trips and falls over a dip in the grass. Yeah, I wish I had been there for that one; I'm nothing if not empathetic. His brother called again; Big Guy stopped and came back like nothing happened.

Our younger autie boy, Little Bear, is also a "runner", but not as adept at it as Big Guy. His advantage is being a planner. When he has a mission, he sets at it. So we're locked up fairly tight around the house, except while barbequing. Little Bear likes to watch from the sliders… and watch…and plan. One day I heard the shout of my aspie boy. Little Bear was outside, barefoot, wandering aimlessly in our fenced yard, probably pondering his success and wondering when we'd figure it out.

He's also a food snatcher. Luckily for him he has younger twin sisters who eats slow. He watches, and plans. When he's finished, but they're not, the food is fair game. Unfortunately for Little Bear, they're verbal and able to alert the authorities. Poor Little Bear, foiled again.

It's a similar scenario when others build block towers. He'll scope it out, circling like a shark. When it gets to a certain height of his choosing he goes for the kill and knocks it right down. Now see, I find that funny. For his siblings, however, it's hit or miss. If only Little Bear would use his gift for good and not evil.

Having two aspie children brings about chuckles as well, at least when they're not fighting. Our oldest daughter is quick with the quips, like when she called Little Bear a "raisin robber". Or when she told her older aspie brother "Don't glare at me, that's Mommy's job!"

So autism is serious business, that's true. But in between the challenges and the tears, there is also plenty of laughter. *I love these kiddos!*

Michele Hughes is mom to six children, two "auties" (16 and 5), two "aspies" (13 and 9), and adorable twins (3), and wife to one, Michael, for 21 years. Her blog is *Living and Learning on the Spectrum* at www.liveandlearnonthespectrum.blogspot.com.

The Gritty Part of Raising a Kid with Autism

By Marjorie Hansen

It's usually the floor. Although you'd be surprised at what they can manage to smear on the walls, and even the ceiling if all the stars align perfectly. Yesterday, however, it was the floor.

While I realize that there are a lot worse things than casually walking into the kitchen and stepping on corn meal, it is thoroughly unpleasant. Fortunately, I managed to avoid slipping on the eggs. At that point, I was grateful that I only had two eggs left in the carton.

I'm not sure what Will was planning on making. But he started with two eggs because he always starts with the eggs. Then he added cornmeal and powdered sugar.

My son Will likes to cook, and he has autism. Those two facts sometimes collide with spectacular and inedible results. But sometimes they collide and I find vegetable faces, piles of chopped up carrots, and the beginning of a cake. And sometimes when they collide, I pull out my silverware drawer and find cornmeal.

Will has cooking phases much the same way Beethoven had musical periods. In William's first phase, the face phase, I'd find faces made out of vegetables and fruit around the house; sometimes on plates, sometimes not. His second phase, the knife phase, was a little disconcerting. He never cut himself, but I wasn't thrilled that my six year old was using a knife unsupervised. The third phase was the egg phase.

Unfortunately, we're still in the egg phase. I think we might always be in the egg phase. On a positive note, at least now about half the time the eggs end up in a bowl. The fourth phase, the plate phase, involved putting favorite ingredients on a plate. Often I'd find marshmallows, peanut butter, chocolate chips, and bananas on a plate. The current and fifth phase is a baking phase.

Will might just be the only kid in the world who actually learned to cook from Steve from *Blue's Clues*. Will watched the banana cake episode over and over again, and memorized the recipe. I walked into the kitchen one day to find bananas and eggs in a bowl. "One cup sugar", Will instructed me. How could I resist that? Surprisingly the cake was pretty good.

In a perfect universe, a cooking college for autistic adults would exist. Will would move into the dorms with his friend Pete, and he would call me weekly. Mostly to complain that he didn't have enough money, but occasionally just to let me know he missed me and to find out what was going on at home.

But I don't live in a perfect universe. Will doesn't have a college education in his future. I'm the one who will teach him how to cook. And I'm not sure he cares about what is going on at home. But in his future I see a lot of cookies, banana cake, and brownies. And yes, his future is tasty!

Marjorie Hansen blogs at www.lifeasthemotherof4. blogspot.com. She enjoys dragging her children to art museums, forcing them to practice the piano, flute, and violin, and do their homework. In her free time she likes to read, eat chocolate, and watch banal TV.

Consider the Magic

By Gina St. Aubin

Basking in the warmth of the midday sun, listening to the deep throaty sounds of a helicopter as its flight pattern runs above our house, I'm struck by the clouds against the blue sky. The depth, the height, the silent floating in unison of one great unknown pattern. They slowly move to the east, giving that slightly dizzying feeling. Where your head feels like it's just a little behind the movement. In an instant, you know your place, your measure against the world, the universe.

Later as the helicopter's song is long gone, as the silence fills my sun-worshiping afternoon, I still find myself looking up to the skies above. This time, it's the airplanes. Silent, foreign, far; too far to make any noise known to me.

It is then that their silent magnificence, the view that J has of them makes sense to me. They are a wonder. These large metal beasts taming the air surrounding them, cutting through the fluff of the clouds carrying people...somewhere. Here. Away. Somewhere.

The fact that such large constructs of metal can do such a thing is wonderfully amazing. It's all the mechanics, the engineering, pure calculations of science, matter and how they all interact...except to a little boy.

To a boy with all the needs of J's, airplanes and all flight machines are a wonder. A construct of hope, awe, magic. I wonder if this is the reason why he loves them so. Why he flies them around our house, mimicking their sound. To pause and consider them? To consider their possibilities? To consider the number of other things that may be possible if hunks of smooth metal can be welded together, painted a pretty color, and thrown into the sky with the normalcy that we all have now taken for granted?

Metal turned to planes, or steaming and storming trains clicking upon a maze of metal, carrying secrets across our path to another place unknown. Powerful enough to smooth our metal monies when laid upon their tracks, to entice thunder in his chest. Thunder of movement coupled with the beating of an excited heart. Oh, the wonders of metal.

If a six year old boy with cerebral palsy, autism, epilepsy, and more can see the magic that our world holds, taking care to point it out at each passing, ensuring we take part in the magic surrounding us, that we don't let it pass us by so easily, shouldn't we watch? Take note. Consider the possibilities our world holds.

Gina St. Aubin is a wife and mother of three, one diagnosed with cerebral palsy, autism, Landau-Kleffner Syndrome, Sensory Processing Disorder, and developmental delays, and is a former victim's advocate now advocating for those with intellectual and physical challenges on her site, *Special Happens*, at www.specialhappens.com.

Ten Things I Wish Somebody Would Have Told Me When My Child Was Diagnosed With Autism

By Katrina Carefoot

The first two years after your child is diagnosed with autism will be the hardest two years of your life. Nobody told me that. I got a lot of "Have you tried this diet?" and "You should see this doctor", which was sometimes helpful, but mostly not. If one of the parents of children with autism who I reached out to for advice had said "Buckle up, Buttercup, this is going to be a rough ride", that would have helped prepare me for what was coming.

For many families, the road to just getting a diagnosis is a long one. Our journey started when our son Max was fourteen months old. He was not officially diagnosed until he was thirty-two months old. So, before we had even arrived at "D-Day", we had been slugging it out for a year and a half.

The diagnosis wasn't a surprise, but it still knocked us on our asses. There was a sense of relief that we finally knew what was wrong with Max, and what we could do to help him. That is what we focused on. Getting him into Applied Behavior Analysis (ABA) therapy right away was our priority. We also had him in speech therapy, occupational therapy, and music therapy. We did *everything* we could to provide him with as much therapy as early on as possible.

As Max's mom, and self-proclaimed leader in our war against autism, I was completely absorbed in every step forward and every step back. Max was the last thing on my mind before a fell asleep each night and the first thing I thought about when I woke up every morning. I had not yet realized that this war is a marathon, not a race. Clearly I could not maintain this pace, something had to change. I needed to put myself first for a little while so that I wouldn't completely fall apart, which wouldn't help anyone, least of all Max.

Now that I have survived the first two years, I have my own advice for families of newly diagnosed children with autism. It goes something like this:

1. This sucks, and I'm sorry that you have joined the autism tribe.

2. The next two years are going to be really hard, and there is no getting around it.

3. You will grieve for the child you thought you had, and feel guilty for wishing your child could be like other kids.

4. You should probably get yourself into therapy too, because you will need it.

5. Make sure you take time for your marriage, or else it will most likely fall apart.

6. Ask for help from friends and family and be specific about what you need.

7. Your child is still awesome and worthy of your love.

8. Celebrate the small wins like they are huge victories.

9. Don't let the setbacks ruin your day.

10. Take time for yourself – that is the biggest gift you can give yourself and your family.

Allowing yourself to fall apart is what is selfish – not making your physical, emotional, and mental health a priority.

And, please know, it gets better. It really does. All you have to do now is remember to breathe.

Katrina writes for the award winning website www.ficklefeline.ca which she founded in 2004. Her candid writing and bare bones honesty have won her accolades from both the mental health and autism communities. She is an autism advocate and is currently documenting her autistic son Max's journey for a book she is writing on how to achieve a best outcome for autism through early intervention and intensive therapy.

How Autism Rocks My World

By D.S. Smith aka Marsupial Mama

As any autie parent will tell you, life with an autistic child can be difficult, draining, and downright soul-crushing at times. Aside from pressing questions like "Will he ever be potty-trained?", "How old is too old to bring my still-in-diapers-boy to the public ladies room with me?", "Can he really survive on just bread and cereal?", and "When is it okay to smack someone openly staring at your frantically stimming child?", there are the practical matters of actually getting someone to listen to you if you're pre-diagnosis (especially if you're a first time parent), booking and showing up to doctor's appointments (especially if you have more than one child), and fighting for services (especially if you live in an area where these are grossly under-developed).

Life is definitely an uphill battle, and I'm often reminded of the study that showed that the stress levels of those parenting an autistic child are comparable to the stress levels of troops fighting on the front line. To say that it's no walk in the park is a joyous understatement. But as hard as life may be with an autistic child, frankly, whose life isn't hard? Who doesn't worry about their future or, more importantly, their children's future? Sure, some people can't seem to catch a break while others appear to have it easy. But for every person that's struggling with seemingly insurmountable challenges, another one comes along whose situation is apparently intent on redefining the term "hell on earth".

While autism undeniably sucks, life with my autistic son does not. And even though thinking "it could be so much worse" does little to help when we're going through bad times, it does make me appreciate the good times so much more than I ordinarily would. I don't need to explain the love any parent has for their child: the unfathomable depth of emotion that overtakes you with the turn of a head and a mischievous smile, or the overwhelming feeling of impotence that crushes you when they're having a particularly difficult time. Such is the emotional roller-coaster of parenthood.

While I would like to be able to eradicate autism from our lives (or even the world), it has dragged up a few blessings through its destructive path. Both my husband and I are more patient, understanding, more forgiving and tolerant. We've become better parents by learning to be more observant about the things that affect our son, and, by extension, the rest of the family. It's really helped us appreciate every milestone, every development, and victory in a way that we probably wouldn't have before. We're better equipped to deal with minor hiccups since we always have to be prepared for a category five storm. We don't, as they say, sweat the small stuff.

And life with an autistic child can just be plain old funny. He's constantly saying things, doing things that are just too cute! And from what I can gather from parents whose autistic children have broken the toddler sound barrier and emerged into childhood or even adolescence, these kids just keep getting cuter, quirkier, and funnier. I mean, yeah, we might struggle with toilet training for much longer than neurotypical kids. But the other side of the coin is that if I'm going to the bathroom and Taz is playing with his toys in the hallway, I can hear him give me a round of applause and say, "Good pee-pee, Mama!", for the successful completion of my task. Just like he gets when he goes.

D. S. Smith is a baby-wearing, co-sleeping, attachment parenting Mama. Taz is 3 ½, on the autism spectrum, and until recently totally non-verbal, and Betty is 7 months old. New to blogging and ASD, she can usually be found tangled up in knitting projects screaming for help. Her blog is *Autism Rocks* at www.autismrocksandrolls.blogspot.com.

Dear Xbox

By Valerie O'Donovan

Xbox: you seemingly innocuous, little black box, how I loathe thee and the fact that I have to perform major surgery just to extricate my son from your tenuous grasp every time I need him to eat his dinner, do his homework, or brush his teeth. You have taken over our house ever since you came into our lives a mere two years ago. You knew what you were doing when you set your sights on our ASD kid, with his love of all things technological, didn't you?

Oh how you lure him into your myriad of games, completely engrossing him so that all he can think and talk about day and night is Xbox and "levels" and "credits" and "glitches". It's very discommoding for a parent to have to call their child ten times and not be heard. There have even been times, dear Xbox, when I've had to step away from my addiction laptop simply to get through to him.

Your games take over the mind as they are re-enacted blow for blow on the trampoline, walking home from school, or even in the shower, so that we're always on the Xbox, even when we're not. They are frustration-invoking, meltdown-making, and argument-inducing nightmares of epic proportions, as my ears are regularly assaulted by tearful protestations such as "*Oh my God, that is so UNFAIR!*"

How you also tire the easily over-loaded ASD kid and cause problems for parents trying to tear them away at night, even though their friends are still playing. In a desperate bid to avoid them being in trouble at school the next day for being lethargic, even though their friends who played for way longer are not. Did you ever consider that, dear Xbox?

However, dear Xbox, there are some functions your little black box provides that are to my liking. My ASD boy loves the Forge function in your Halo games where he can "make his own maps" and "build his own bases". I love to see him use his acute visual spatial skills, and work on his organization and planning ones whilst doing so. I also rather enjoy seeing all his military style vehicles neatly lined up in a row.

Your Xbox Live experience, whilst introducing him to some choice profane language, also expands his social world by including it in his technological one. Oh, dear Xbox, how I love these social skills opportunities!

How he learns by invitation as he gets to give and receive "invites to the party" and how to ask nicely to join a game already in play. How he also learns to play nice, and how to deal with bullies and mean players. If someone is not playing nice he can just "block them" or "boot them out" (his words!). If only that, ahem, could be as easily applied in real life!

The opportunities for team building and strategy planning are huge as I hear them all working together towards a common goal. I can almost forgive the fact that said common goal usually involves dead creatures!

Have you any idea, dear Xbox, the way my heart sings when the last thing he does before we go away on holiday and the first when we return is to go on Xbox to greet his friends? How happy it made me when he once apologized for playing longer than agreed, as he had received so many invites from his friends on his return! Social inclusion and acceptance is a wonderful thing to behold, dear Xbox.

Unfortunately, there are also opportunities to fall out with one's friends on Xbox, just as in real life. However did you realize, dear Xbox, that aforementioned map-making facilities can also be used to facilitate a reconciliation? Yep. Shapes can be used to spell out words you know. Like the word "sorry" for example. A very big, proud mummy moment that was!

To conclude, dear Xbox, I feel the overall Xbox experience is a good one. We will therefore tolerate your little black box in our house for a while longer, under strict agreed playing conditions of course.

Valerie O'Donovan lives in Dublin, Ireland with her husband and son, who is on the autism spectrum. She is a stay-at-home-mum who, as well as running the home and raising the wonderful WiiBoy, also enjoys dancing and choreographing. Although a technophobe, she is a complete social media butterfly, as she flutters between Twitter, Facebook, and her blog. She blogs as Jazzygal at www.jazzygals-steppingout.blogspot.com, where she serves up all of her rambling ruminations with a side of humor.

A Line of Their Own

By Tessa Jordan

Like most parents who have young children, my husband and I spend a lot of time stepping over and around toys. With four kids and a few overindulgent grandparents, our house is a giant toy box bursting at the seams with stuffed animals, Hot Wheels, and My Little Ponies.

We try to contain the chaos as much as possible, but the massive collection of kid paraphernalia inevitably finds its way back to its "home" spot on the floor. You see, three of our four children have autism spectrum disorders, and the expression, "A place for everything, and everything in its place," has a different meaning in our house.

Children with autism can be quirky, no doubt about it. Yet, even though they might share certain traits each child is utterly unique. Their individuality shines through, even in the stereotyped behaviors of autism, which includes an obsessive need to line up and arrange objects.

My son Elijah is nine years old, and he has Asperger's Syndrome. His world is black and white. Rules are made to never be broken, and routines are adhered to with militant precision. When he plays with his Transformers or army men, he lines them up in perfect formation. Six across, five rows deep, each figure spaced exactly apart from the others. He doesn't need a ruler. His eyes can detect the slightest irregularity in his design. And like his approach to everything else in life, once he's done, he's done. The formation is forgotten and he moves on to something else, not caring if it gets demolished in his absence.

Our daughter Lela, on the other hand, is much more fluid in her lining-up obsession. She creates arcs and long snaking lines. She is our most adaptable child, and her lack of precision reflects that. However, she's also my most fragile. Her lines may not be perfectly straight, but no one should go anywhere near them!

Noah, our youngest, is our wild child. He careens through life at ninety miles per hour, utterly fearless and determined to climb every piece of furniture in our house. His line of Hot Wheels are as on-the-go as he is. He loves to squeeze his cars into seemingly impossible places. It's not uncommon to open a door in our house and find a row of cars that have been shoved under the door. Noah does what I like to call speed-lining. He uses the same five Hot Wheels, arranging them side by side as if they've just done that really cool hit the brakes and slide sideways maneuver. Once they're all lined up, he gives a squeal and a flap of his hands, and then he's off again, moving them to a different table or counter top. Noah likes everything in his life to follow a routine, but for what he's passionate about there are no limits or boundaries.

My children share a diagnosis of a neurological disorder, but even though they exhibit common traits, they are still individuals. They have distinct personalities. Autism does not suppress who they are, and it doesn't define who they will become. Like any child, the future is wide open for them. I don't know exactly what it will entail, but I do know this: their road of life might be straightforward and clear, full of twists and turns, or veer into completely unchartered territory, but their father and I will be there every step of the way. However, their life will be their own.

Tessa Jordan is a teacher, advocate, and mom to four amazing children. She and her husband Joe have been married for twelve years. They enjoy a hectic, joyful life in north Louisiana. When she isn't busy being driven crazy by her children, Tessa enjoys reading novels, writing poetry, and fantasizing that her house will someday get cleaned. She blogs at www.applesandautobots.blogspot.com.

Think Before You Speak!

By Caryn Black Haluska

Living at the Monster House provides plenty of fodder for blogging – the good, the bad, and the ugly. There is always a funny little anecdote, drama, or story that starts out "I can't make up stuff this good!"

With seven monsters running around, there is also a constant stream of conversation coming from my end, as the mother. I've said things I never dreamed would come out of my mouth including, but not limited to, "Stop table dancing, you're underage!", "The sensory table is NOT a buffet!", "Don't pick your brother's nose, it's rude!", and "No, pimple-puss is not a curse word."

Having a child on the autism spectrum just makes life that much more interesting. It doesn't seem to matter that he has a speech delay, as he is more than making up for it now.

About a month ago, I noticed Logan had developed an uncanny ability to hear something only once, and then use it appropriately, never deviating from it. For example, one day he wanted to sit by me on the back step during play time. He growled "MOVE!" about four hundred times, making it clear that my posterior was taking up more room that he deemed necessary. I explained to him that we say "Excuse me" instead of "MOVE!" He has never once done it again. He will, however, climb up behind me on the desk chair when I work on the computer, and growl "Excuse me!" followed by a ferocious "THANK YOU!" when I move over. The boy is nothing if not polite.

Likewise, he will pick up things I say to the other monsters. Lately, there has been a problem with cursing in our happy monster home. I found myself admonishing "Don't say that!" several times a day with my teenage monsters, until one day before I could repeat it once again, Logan growled, "DON'T SAY THAT!" I sat back and let my two year old take care of it. The teen monsters were delighted that their Logan was allowed to discipline in this way, and Logan feels like the king of the heap.

This doesn't work as well, however, when it's Daddy cursing imaginatively at his internet connection, his frozen computer, his tools, his phone, lack of toilet paper, etc. Daddy was not delighted with Logan knocking on his bedroom door and growling "DON'T SAY THAT!" But the rest of us thought it was hysterical.

Logan's newest love is following around #4. This girl is the eleven year old drama queen of all drama queens. If she thinks you're being melodramatic about something, she'll sneer, "Oh, sniffle. Oh, tear." and trace an imaginary tear trail down her cheek. This drives me batty. She came home from a play date recently and was moaning about how no one loved her, she has no friends, her life is horrible, I'm the meanest mother in the world, and on and on and on. Logan heard her pitiful wailing and walked right up to her, called her by name, and said, "Oh, sniffle. Oh, tear." and traced an imaginary tear trail down his cheek. I don't think I've ever seen her shut up quite so fast. Note to self: carry video camera at all times.

Caryn Black Haluska is the mother of seven cuddly monsters. When her youngest was diagnosed with Sensory Processing Disorder and Pervasive Developmental Disorder, she channeled her copywriting experience into blogging at www.livingwithlogan.com where she shares glimpses into the amusing antics at the Monster House, as well as information about interventions, gluten-free/casein-free (GFCF) cooking, and the importance of family. Caryn shares the ups and downs of living with special needs children in her unique voice that will inspire you to look at your own monster house through new eyes.

Why I Have Learned To Be an Optimist and Positive Thinker in Life with Autism

By Floortime Lite Mama

I have learned to be an optimist in my special needs life. It's interesting to me that prior to my special needs life I had a tendency to be a pessimist.

In my special needs world, I usually meet with two types of responses to my continued focus on optimism and hope.

Most people say that they feel encouraged when they read my essays. But some people tell me that they find my perspective unrealistic and unbelievable. That either I just pretend to be happy, or that my son has the light version of autism.

Though these assumptions are untrue, these questions have made me reflect on why I think positivity has a critical role in autism parenting.

First, perception is everything. Autism for many of us – certainly for my family – is here to stay. While we cannot change that fact, we can certainly change the way we look at it.

Second, R's life is about him and not about me. And what is most important is that *he* sees his life as happy and useful. And that he sees himself as worthy. And I can contribute to his self-worth every moment making sure that he sees a beautiful reflection of himself in my eyes.

Third, the way we look at R influences all the people around him, for the non-autistic world is profoundly socially-referential.

Fourth, while I really do understand and empathize, I think that thinking about the life I may have had with a neurotypical child is a waste of time. In fact, thinking of all alternate realities is a waste of time. Besides if we want to think of alternate realities, why do we never think of negative alternate realities? Why do we only imagine the good things that could have happened and did not?

The only life to be lived is the one we are in. And the only child to love is the one we have.

Fifth, a positive outlook makes me believe that intelligence and ability are present. Even if that ability is hard to access, when we believe in its presence, we work harder to find it. Interestingly, we usually find what we look for – whether it be a strength or a deficit.

And finally, the present is as important as a future. And optimism has a magical effect on the way we experience today.

So these are all these logical, rational reasons why I believe positivity has great value in autism parenting. But beyond the *logic*, there is the *art* of living a happy life in which optimism is critical. Awareness that this is the only life we have. And that each day wasted in worry, regret, and fear is a day forever gone. And that there is a way of looking at your child, autism and all, as though they were an incredible gift. And a way of seeing yourself as unbelievably lucky.

And so that is what I do.

And I hope I stay optimistic forever.

Floortime Lite Mama is the mother of an adorable 6 year old autistic child and blogs at www.drycappucino. blogspot.com.

My Kid Is on the Spectrum, But Your Kid is Just Weird

By Flannery Sullivan

It takes time to recover from receiving an autism spectrum diagnosis for your child. Parents will go through the stages of grief, and will spend countless hours doing research, trying different interventions, and reading books about spectrum disorders. Eventually it consumes every waking moment of your life, leaving you exhausted, both mentally and physically.

This is what I did, and after some time, I decided to step back and take a break. This is the point where I began to realize that the world hasn't come to an end, and my son is making progress, albeit slowly, but steady progress nonetheless.

By this time he was school age, giving me more opportunities to observe the other children at school.

And what I noticed from observing them is that they are freaks.

Little Susie can already read and write beautifully, but she's also obsessed with princesses, and pitches a fit if her shoes aren't covered in colorful glitter. "But Princess Jasmine ALWAYS wears glitter shoes!" I don't care how hot she grows up to be, this is going to be one major high maintenance Paris Hilton wannabe if she's all about the bling in kindergarten.

Little Johnnie has lots of friends, which is odd, because on the playground he's a bully. I know he's a bully because he snatched the hat off my kid's head, and my kid smacked him in the face. My kid got in trouble, of course, even though he was the one picked on, and has a disability. Ironically, I totally would have bitch-slapped little Johnnie too if he snatched the hat off my head. So was it an autism behavior or an "I'm not going to put up with your crap" behavior?

There are three lovely little girls over there. Two are picking on the other one, because she's playing with a toy pony that they wanted. They've decided to shun and tease her. They are supposedly *normal*. However, their *normal* is frighteningly similar to the pack behavior of wild orangutans, except nobody is doing any social grooming.

My kid, on the other hand, actually tries to play with others, and doesn't understand when they yell at each other or say mean things. He doesn't understand because he's on the spectrum, and he doesn't know how to tease. He knows all about being bossy and rigid, and trying to make the kids play what he wants to play, over and over again until they can't take it anymore. And sure, he might run into my room every morning when I'm getting dressed, honk my boobs, and then run out... but he's not mean.

The long and short of it is that I've come to accept my son just as he is, without analyzing and questioning every little behavior. One person's hissy fit about glitter shoes is another's rigidity and insistence at singing "I eat smelly bugs" instead of "Feliz Navidad". The only difference is that only one of us has to worry about offending the Hispanic neighbors. The other has to worry about getting that chick married off someday.

Flannery Sullivan is a native of Southern California. She and her family currently reside in the country of Texas, and look forward to visiting their native country in the near future. With a firm belief that there is humor in all things, Flannery writes about raising a child on the spectrum at www.theconnorchronicles.wordpress.com. Her hobbies include sticking out like a sore thumb, rocking boats, and raging against machines.

Dancing To the Beat of a Different Drummer

By Lynn Hudoba

As awareness of autism increases, there are a growing number of activities geared towards people with autism. A major theater chain now schedules sensory-friendly movie nights, as do some museums and indoor playgrounds. Park districts have long provided special needs versions of their programs, including sports, summer camps, and community outings.

My seven year old daughter has autism, and has participated in nearly all of these activities. And while I am so grateful that they are available, parents are also strongly encouraged to expose their autistic children to "typical" peers as much as possible. Especially if a child is in a self-contained classroom all day with other autistic children, it is considered to be beneficial to have them around typical children so that they can model their behaviors and play skills. So my daughter has attended typical summer camps, and, most recently, a ballet class. She does so with the support of a one-on-one aid that helps her to stay on task and facilitates social interaction with the other children.

Although my daughter has some gross motor issues and has difficulty getting her body to do what she wants it to do, she absolutely loved her ballet class. More than half the attraction was in wearing the leotard, tights, toe shoes, and tutu. But she also seemed to love the music, the teacher, and watching all of the other little girls in her class. She had every right to be frustrated when she couldn't dance all of the steps or maintain the positions as her classmates did, but she was undeterred and seemed to thrill to every minute of it. She insisted on wearing her ballet outfit during nearly all of her afterschool waking hours, and endlessly showed off the first five positions that she had mastered.

When it came time for the final class, parents were invited to attend for a mini-recital. All of them were lined up in the audience like paparazzi, with cameras, cell phones, and video recorders planted in front of their faces. If they didn't know by then that there was a special needs student in their child's class, they were soon to find out.

Audrey was surely dancing to the beat of a different drummer that night, as she struggled to keep up and drifted precariously close to the adjacent ballerinas.

I could have cringed at the reaction of the other parents or at the thought of how many of their pictures and movies she was wandering into, but instead I chose to focus on the positive. The moves did not come naturally to her and the invasion of the others' personal space was due to the fact that she was concentrating so hard on the teacher's instructions that she lost her awareness of those around her.

She caught sight of me at one point during the recital and, momentarily forgetting about the task at hand, rushed over to give me a hug. She was so happy and excited and proud of herself, and I reciprocated those emotions entirely.

Lynn Hudoba is the mother of an amazing 7 year old girl, who happens to have autism. Her blog is *My Life as an Ungraceful, Unhinged, and Unwilling Draftee into the Autism Army*, and can be found at www.autismarmymom.com. Follow her and her daughter as they take the road less traveled, dance to a different drummer, and lots of other clichés that describe their unique, unexpected, and often hilarious journey.

How Long?

By Brian

Don't get me wrong. I love my almost 4 year old autistic son more than I love myself. There is literally almost nothing I won't do for him. The list of things I have done for him includes many things that I will not list here. It's long and almost always disgusting. To put the list here would probably be inappropriate. No, scratch that. Definitely inappropriate.

We also have a wonderful, beautiful, active, social, typical daughter who is nearing her second birthday. There also is literally almost nothing I won't do for her. Unfortunately, with the demands of autism and her brother, there are a lot of things that seem unfair to her.

The perfect example happened recently. I was finishing a baseball game on the TV, and she was patiently waiting for it to finish. (Note: she really didn't care what was on TV, as long as it wasn't Elmo.) Finally, my Cubbies pulled defeat out of the jaws of victory again, and it was time to play.

"Time to play, guys!" my melodic, radio-quality voice rang across the house. Gracie came running, smiling the entire way to her room, the location of the toys. Just then, I heard the sound of a chair in the kitchen, rubbing its felt pads on the wooden floor, making its inevitable trek towards the cupboard and the tasty cookies inside. Two kids, one desperately wanting attention, the other needing correction. I made my choice, and retrieved AJ from the no-no, where he got mad, ran, stomped, and threw a mini-fit.

This lasted about three minutes. When the situation was resolved, I had almost forgotten about playtime. Walking into the room, I saw my wonderful daughter, sitting patiently, pointing at her toys and saying "please", eyes shining with delight. My heart broke.

All is well right now with the siblings, who absolutely adore one another. But with situations like this, situations that require my daughter to wait, how long? How long until patience runs thin and resentment blooms? How long will it be until she stops waiting? How long will it be until she feels we favor her brother? How long will she love him, and forgive the minor slights we give her? How long will she put up with his occasional tantrums, and awful pinching?

How long?

After their son was diagnosed with autism, Brian and his wife started reading numerous autism blogs and couldn't help but join in. They offer their unique perspectives – his silly stories, her witty insights – and often discuss topics in "Both Sides" posts, giving a father's versus mother's take on life as a special needs parent. You can find their blog at www.bothsidesofthecoin1.blogspot.com.

The Suspense is Killing Me!

By Jean Myles

My three year old on the spectrum used to blurt out that phrase all too often. There was no meaning behind it, just echolalia (repetition of phrases) at its finest. Ming-Ming from the Nick Jr. show *Wonder Pets* was to blame for that gem and although it was out of place and awkward, we cherished him saying anything. He rarely spoke any words until he was two and a half, and even then it was about 95% echolalia.

As I fought with the car seat buckle every day after ABA therapy, I asked "How was your day?" His reply, "How was your day?" Simply an imitation, not a return of pleasantries.

My baby's inability to tell me what he did and how he felt about it was one of the hardest things about him being non-verbal. The only glimpse I had of what he did all day in ABA therapy was a yellow sheet of paper describing his discrete trial tests – stacking blocks, naming animals, pointing to objects, lacing beads.

Some of those early phrases were random, but echolalia is also a way for kids on the spectrum to communicate. I literally ran the car off the road one day when I got a response to a question I always asked without even a hint of a comeback.

"What did you have for snack?"

"Do you want cheese balls or pretzels?"

"Wait! Were those your choices today? Is that what your teacher asked? Which one did you pick? I am so proud of you!"

My screams of excitement and rapid fire questions probably made him wish he remained silent. In fact, I now wonder if he would have spoken more and sooner had I not jumped all over him like a baboon in heat each time he uttered a sound. I had no idea whether he chose cheese balls or pretzels, and didn't really care; I just reveled in having a vague idea of what my baby was eating for snack!

With my body shoved halfway into the fireplace as I struggled to build a fire one evening, he came around behind me, put his hand on my back and very seriously said, "Mom, we have a compsognathus problem."

Thank you Dino Dan, for giving my son words to convey that he understood my frustration. Whether it was building a fire or ridding our home of small bird-like dinosaurs is not important; we were communicating.

I realized echolalia has also rubbed off on our neu-rotypical two year old when they both walked by me a few days ago and in dead pan dialogue without cracking a smile recited:

"Liar!"

"He's not lying, he speaks the truth."

What the heck are they watching anyway?

My son now nears the age of five and he is fully ver-bal, a miracle I am thankful for each day, but echolalia still lives on. Sometimes it is meaningful, an intention on his part to tell me something in the best way he can, but other times it is still completely out of left field.

While putting him to bed recently he said to my hus-band, "Dad, thanks for the haircut today."

I gushed over the sweetness and waited patiently to receive my term of sentiment. "Mom, we are going to need three and a half capfuls."

What? Repeating a line from *Team Umizoomi*? Help-ing to make sure I do the laundry correctly? Or in his, a brilliant and completely endearing way of thanking me for all the work I put in that day to take care of him.

Jean Myles is a freelance writer, marketing executive, former teacher, and mommy to two boys, one on the autism spectrum. You can find her at www.MommyToTwoBoys.com.

The Power of Obsession

By Meredith Vale

I believe that the energy crisis would be solved if it was possible to harness the power of autistic obsessions. I have personally been likened to a tornado of obsessive energy, and yet I stand in awe of the single-minded passion my son has for his "special interests". You like that term? "Special interest" is the PC-friendly description of a consuming obsession that is common among autistic individuals.

My son, Louis, was diagnosed as autistic before he was two years old. He is now nearly five. I have been lucky enough to have had my eyes opened to a whole new world. If you don't already know, autistic children are really impressive. They could teach a Zen monk a thing or two about living in the moment. They work so hard at joining us in our obtuse and confusing social world. They speak volumes without saying a word. Quite frankly, I may be biased, but I believe that every family should have one.

Where was I? Oh yes, obsessions. Louis is currently obsessed with dinosaurs. He may not care to sound out the alphabet for you, but give him a chance and he will impart such detailed knowledge about the mating habits of a the female stygymoloch that your head will spin. Then he will act it out. You can't pay for that kind of entertainment. Truly!

Admittedly, being a less focused human being, I have found the endless hooting, head butting, and nest building difficult at times. The irritation usually occurs around 4:00 am when he lies sobbing in my arms because "the dinosaurs are all stink". I am assuming he meant extinct. But there is nothing in the world that compares to watching a slightly-built four year old climbing on his Nanna's back to "mate" and then pointing her to the corner to "lay her eggs".

His passion for dinosaurs is boundless. He is the only four year old I know who eschews the delights of Dora for three hour documentaries on fossil extraction in the arctic. The first thing we hear in the morning is the mournful hoot of the diplodocus over the baby monitor as he lets us know he his awake.

And yet, there was an even greater time. A time of endless hilarity (on my part) and incredible focus (on his). This was the period when Louis was obsessed with windscreen wipers. You may ask, what is there to be excited about in windscreen wipers? Well my friend, have you ever given yourself over to the metronome swish of two wiper blades offset against the rhythmic drumming of the rain? It is a sensory paradise!

And so for a long time windscreen wipers featured large in our family life. Louis even adapted his windscreen techniques to fend off sweet old ladies in shops. I should point out here that sweet old ladies are indeed on Louis' list of nemeses. You see they have a tendency to lean in close and look in his eyes. Louis does NOT approve of strangers taking liberties with his personal space. However, he was always polite and simply frowned at the floor until they went away. That was until he discovered windscreen wipers.

Now as the sweet old dear leans down to gush about how gorgeous he is, he glances up with a beatific smile and raises his arms out, crooked at the elbow. Then he simply swishes them past his face and *wipes* the woman from his view...and calmly moves on. It is really undeniable that there is much power indeed to these obsessions, and we neurotypicals have much to learn.

Meredith Vale is the proud mother of a fabulous autistic boy, and has the support of a loving husband and a brilliant family. When she is not re-enacting scenes from the Discovery Channel, she can be found reading, blogging, and talking about autism. Meredith is slogging through a degree in special education and disability studies and embraces any opportunity that encourages inclusion, support, and respect for differently-abled people. Her blog is www.andsoitgoes_louisandhenry.blogspot.com.

Welcome to Asperger's Island

By Kara Wilson

I, like many PBS viewers, have always had it in for Rick Steves. My commitment to disdain for his experiences grew exponentially with the birth of my daughter, for we were essentially sequestered to our home during her first three years. While Rick enjoyed the rich culture, cuisine, and history of Andalucía, I was hoping I might one day see the inside of a Target again.

Then it dawned on me that bitterness is not the answer. Mr. Steves may have the inside track to all of Europe, but I imagined one day he'd watch my travel show where I provide a personal tour to our family's Asperger's, the Northern-most island of the Autism Keys. And it goes a little somethin' like this (cue exotic background music, but not too loudly):

Hi, I'm Kara Wilson. In this episode of *Travels*, I will take you on an incredible adventure to an island of distinctive style. It's a place full of customs and culture, where all of your senses will be awakened, but not over-stimulated.

Our journey begins with your arrival at the island's humble estate. Enter the grand foyer where you will witness the unique placement of items moveable by a four year old, from sunflower seeds to furniture. The lining up of seemingly ordinary things is considered sacred and should be left undisturbed. Feel free to take pictures, but use of a flash is not allowed.

Our gift shop is stocked with specialty items and souvenirs. Headphones, pressure vests, tag-less clothing, timers, and thermometers are just some of the amenities we offer. Watches are also available, but if you'd rather ask the time every two minutes, that's okay too. Exact change is appreciated in the event our four year old clerk is not fond of your facial hair and won't talk to you.

Your lavish accommodations include a white noise machine. Rooms with large swings and trampolines are available for a nominal fee. You may ring the front desk one time, and one time only to ask if it's morning. It won't be and you will be returned to your room until the sun rises. We ask that you refrain from using restroom facilities for the duration of your stay as flushing toilets and the use of hand dryers is strictly prohibited.

The island flora, insects, and bird species will be described with a passion and finesse unique to our experienced guide. Please refrain from questions until the end of each tour. Or, better yet, just keep them to yourselves, as it's oftentimes difficult to determine when the end actually occurs. It is recommended you do your best not to nod off during any portion of the ninety-minute tours.

Enjoy fresh, local cuisine where our in-house chef will prepare the same meal for you throughout the duration of your stay. Menu items include: eight ounce glasses of milk warmed for forty-five seconds in the microwave, crispy tortillas with light brown spots, sliced apples with cinnamon, fresh-shelled snap peas, nothing with mushrooms or stinky cheese, and all desserts under the sun. Rest assured, nothing on your plate will touch.

We hope you enjoy your visit to this eccentric destination, and may you overlook the fact that the island parents often times look frazzled, don't speak in full sentences, and sometimes drool. This merely adds to the authenticity of your experiences.

Until next time, I'm Kara. And Rick, should you and I ever have the opportunity to one day cross paths during our travels, I'll do my best to avoid ninja chopping your European-traveling Eustachian tubes.

Kara Wilson is a never-humorless mother to an extremely wise 4 year old daughter with Asperger's

Syndrome, who is akin to parenting a grandmother at times. While there's never a dull moment, it is both exhausting and lovely. She is her joy. Kara blogs at www. karacteristic.com.

Proving Me Wrong

By Jessica Watson

Stepping onto the bus she barely catches her coat as it hits the step.

I fold my arms a bit tighter, holding back the urge to swoop in and help.

She had followed her list perfectly, filling her new bag with folders and pencils and a squishy ball (just in case).

The bag was so heavy she tilted as she walked. Wanting to take it off her shoulder, I refold my arms instead.

This year was different.

She didn't want me to drop her off or walk her into her classroom.

Talking to her teacher about food allergies and sensory needs and the fact that I was scared to death she would never be able to open a locker would have to be done out of her range.

High school was upon us and she wanted to tackle it just like everyone else: without her mom.

I held my breath and hoped that I had done enough.

Could we really do this? Who decided she was ready? And who in the world decided I was ready?

High school hallways are packed and loud and chaotic, everything we had avoided for the last fourteen years.

And those kids that go to high school? They are almost adults.

They speak for themselves, count out their lunch money and keep track of their own homework.

I needed to do these things for her, but maybe she was ready to do them on her own.

It took everything I had those first few weeks of school to not call the teacher, email the autism support specialist, and stalk the hallways in disguise making sure she was navigating high school okay.

And now the year is almost over.

She has done it.

We have done it.

Somehow I managed to let her go and she hasn't looked back.

Muddling through jammed lockers and forgotten homework and a lunch account without enough money to even buy a drink, we have survived.

The lessons in letting go that high school have taught me are invaluable.

So many times I have thought that there are things that my daughter cannot do without me, and so many times she has proved me wrong.

To think that ten years ago, I was arguing with our school district about placing her in a kindergarten class, even if she wasn't potty trained or couldn't tie her shoes, keeping to myself the fact that I was scared out of my mind to let her go.

Never in my wildest dreams did I think she would be attending high school, spending half of her day in general education, and forbidding me from waiting at the bus stop after the first day of school.

I worry about her future. I have no idea if she will ever be able to drive or live on her own or hold a job where she feels valued and accepted, and it scares me that there is so much uncertainty.

But I know the future holds just as many surprises as kindergarten and high school, and I look forward to her proving me wrong many, many more times.

Jessica Watson is a writer and mother to five. Her oldest, a daughter with PDD-NOS, inspires her with her courage and strength each and every day. Jessica and her family live in Michigan and you can find her blog at www.fourplusanangel.com.

WANT MORE????

Big Daddy Has a Book Too!

He's been called, "The Dave Barry of Autism Parenting..."

He's also been called "morbidly obese," "ego-maniacal" and "kind of gross."

In the tradition of the great dads of our time...

~Mike Brady, Charlie Sheen, and Homer Simpson~

Big Daddy's hilarious and poignant book gives a peek into how this special needs father turns adversity on its head and makes the most of his life with his autistic son.

Big Daddy's Tales from the Lighter Side of Raising a Kid with Autism

Big Daddy's Tales from the Lighter side of Raising a Kid with Autism is about acceptance more than anything else. Sure there are a ton of poop, fart, and booger stories in there. But mainly Big Daddy shares how his family uses creativity, humor, and acceptance to overcome adversity.

Interested? Of course you are. Get your copy at Amazon.com or at Big Daddy's blog, www.bigdaddyautism. com. A Kindle version is also available.

Made in the USA
Charleston, SC
22 September 2016